Contents

Introduction to the series

Since the introduction of the revised post-16 qualifications (AS and A2 level) in the UK in September 2000, the number of students taking A Level Film and Media Studies has increased significantly. For example, the latest entry statistics show the following trend:

Subject & Level	June 2001	June 2002	June 2004
A Level Film Studies†	2,017	—	—
AS Level Film Studies	3,852	—	7,996
A2 Level Film Studies	—	2,175	4,161
A Level Media Studies*†	16,293	—	—
AS Level Media Studies*	22,872	—	30,745
A2 Level Media Studies*	—	18,150	22,746

*Three combined awarding bodies' results
† Legacy syllabi – last entry June 2001
(*bfi* Education website – AS/A2 statistics refer to cashed-in entries only)

In September 2006, a new A Level specification (syllabus), Moving Image Arts (offered by the Northern Ireland awarding body, CCEA), will be available throughout the UK and it is likely to attract even more students to this lively and popular subject area. We will be adding reference to it in the Assessment contexts section of the forthcoming titles in the series.

Inevitably this increase in student numbers has led to a pressing demand for more teachers. But, given the comparatively recent appearance of both subjects at degree level (and limited availability of specialist post-graduate teaching courses), both new and experienced teachers from other disciplines are faced with teaching these subjects for the first time, without a degree-level background to help them with subject content and conceptual understanding.

In addition, these specifications saw the arrival of new set topics and areas of study, some of which change frequently, so there is a pressing need for up-to-date resources to help teacher preparation, as well as continuing professional development courses.

I meet a large number of Film and Media Studies teachers every year in the course of my various roles and developed the concept and format of this series with the above factors, and busy and enthusiastic teachers, in mind. Each title provides an accessible reference resource, with essential topic content, as well as clear guidance on good classroom practice to improve the quality of teaching and students' learning. We are confident that, as well as supporting the teacher new to these subjects, the series provides the experienced specialist with new critical perspectives and teaching approaches as well as useful content.

The two sample schemes of work included in Section 1 are intended as practical models to help get teachers started. They are not prescriptive, as any effective scheme of work has to be developed with the specific requirements of an assessment context, and ability of the teaching group, in mind. Likewise, the worksheets provided in the online materials offer examples of good practice, which can be adapted to your specific needs and contexts. In some cases, the online resources include additional resources, such as interviews and illustrative material, available as webnotes. See www.bfi.org.uk/tfms.

The series is clear evidence of the range, depth and breadth of teacher expertise and specialist knowledge required at A Level in these subjects. Also, it is an affirmation of why this subject area is such an important, rich and compelling one for increasing numbers of 16- to 19-year-old students. Many of the more theoretical titles in the series include reference to practical exercises involving media production skills. It is important that it is understood here that the current A Levels in Media and Film Studies are not designed as vocational, or pre-vocational, qualifications. In these contexts, the place of practical media production is to offer students active, creative and engaging ways in which to explore theory and reflect on their own practice.

It has been very gratifying to see that the first titles in this series have found an international audience, in the USA, Canada and Australia, among others, and we hope that future titles continue to be of interest in international moving image education.

Every author in the series is an experienced practitioner of Film and/or Media Studies at this level and many have examining/moderating experience. It has been a pleasure to work closely with such a diverse range of committed professionals and I should like to thank them for their individual contributions to this expanding series.

Vivienne Clark
Series Editor
March 2005

● Key features

- Assessment contexts for the major UK post-16 Film and Media Studies specifications
- Suggested schemes of work
- Historical contexts (where appropriate)
- Key facts, statistics and terms
- Detailed reference to the key concepts of Film and Media Studies
- Detailed case studies
- Glossaries
- Bibliographies
- Student worksheets, activities and resources (available online) – ready for you to print and photocopy for the classroom.

● Other titles available in the series include:

Teaching Scriptwriting, Screenplays and Storyboards for Film and TV Production (Mark Readman);
Teaching TV Sitcom (James Baker);
Teaching Digital Video Production (Pete Fraser and Barney Oram;
Teaching TV News (Eileen Lewis);
Teaching Women and Film (Sarah Gilligan);
Teaching World Cinema (Kate Gamm);
Teaching TV Soaps (Lou Alexander and Alison Cousens);
Teaching Contemporary British Broadcasting (Rachel Viney);
Teaching Contemporary British Cinema (Sarah Casey Benyahia);
Teaching Music Video (Pete Fraser).

● Forthcoming titles include:

Teaching Men and Film; *Teaching Analysis of Film Language and Production*; *Teaching Video Games*; *Teaching Film Censorship and Controversy*; *Teaching Stars and Performance*; *Teaching TV Drama*; *Teaching Analysis of Television Language and Production*; *Teaching Short Films*; *Teaching Music and the Moving Image.*

SERIES EDITOR: Vivienne Clark is a former Head of Film and Media Studies and an Advanced Skills Teacher. She is currently an Associate Tutor of *bfi* Education and Principal Examiner for A Level Media Studies for one of the English awarding bodies. She is a freelance teacher trainer, media consultant and writer/editor, with several published textbooks and resources, including *GCSE Media Studies* (Longman 2002), *Key Concepts & Skills for Media Studies* (Hodder Arnold 2002). She is also a course tutor for the *bfi*/Middlesex University MA level module, An Introduction to Media Education, and a link tutor and visiting lecturer for the Central School of Speech & Drama PGCE (Media with English), London.

AUTHORS:

David Wharton has been a teacher since 1991. He was formerly Subject Co-ordinator for Media Studies and is currently Subject Co-ordinator for Film Studies at Gateway Sixth Form College, Leicester. He has delivered workshops in Film Authorship for the *bfi*, and examines A Level Film Studies for an British awarding body.

Jeremy Grant has taught in Spain, Poland and the UK. He currently works at Gateway Sixth Form College, Leicester, where he has delivered courses in Film, English and Media Studies since 2000.

1

Introduction

Assessment contexts

Awarding body & level	Subject	Unit code	Module/Topic
✓ AQA A2	Media Studies	Module 4	Texts and Contexts in the Media
✓ AQA A2	Media Studies	Module 5	Independent Study
✓ OCR A2	Media Studies	2733	Advanced Production
✓ OCR A2	Media Studies	2734	Critical Research Study
✓ OCR A2	Media Studies	2735	Media Issues and Debates
✓ WJEC A2	Media Studies	ME4	Investigating Media Texts
✓ WJEC A2	Media Studies	ME5	Changing Media Industries
✓ WJEC AS	Film Studies	FS1	Making Meaning 1
✓ WJEC AS	Film Studies	FS2	Producers and Audiences
✓ WJEC A2	Film Studies	FS3	British Cinema: Messages and Values
✓ WJEC A2	Film Studies	FS4	Making Meaning 2
✓ WJEC A2	Film Studies	FS5	Studies in World Cinema
✓ WJEC A2	Film Studies	FS6	Critical Studies
✓ CCEA AS	Moving Image Arts	Unit 3	Film Fiction
✓ SQA Higher	Media Studies	DF14 12	Media Analysis: Fiction
✓ SQA Advanced Higher	Media Studies	D332 13	Media Analysis
✓ SQA Advanced Higher	Media Studies	D37A 13	Media Investigation

This guide is also relevant to the following specifications, as well as to international and Lifelong Learning courses: AQA, Ed-Excel, OCR – GNVQ and AVCE media and communication and BTEC National Diploma.

Other guides in this series offer excellent complementary information to this pack:

- *Teaching World Cinema* (Kate Gamm)
- *Teaching Women and Film* (Sarah Gilligan)
- *Teaching Men and Film* (forthcoming)
- *Teaching Analysis of Film Language and Production* (forthcoming)

In addition to its principal intended use as a guide for A Level teaching and equivalent international courses, some or all of this guide will be valuable at undergraduate level, particularly for students who have no previous experience of Film Studies at A2 Level, or perhaps have only studied film as one module on a Media Studies course. It should also be helpful to anyone preparing to deliver a film appreciation leisure course.

● Specification links

AQA Media Studies A2 – Module 4: Texts and Contexts in the Media
Debate about authorship is an integral element in understanding the institutions involved in cinema production.

AQA Media Studies A2 – Module 5: Independent Study
Film authorship is an appropriate issue for study in this unit. Any of the case studies (though the texts are not sufficiently recent for actual use given this specification's requirement of very contemporary texts) will provide useful models of secondary research for this element. Some provide primary research. The resource as a whole provides a good theoretical context.

OCR Media Studies A2 – 2733 Advanced Production
Knowledge and understanding of issues concerning film authorship will support students writing their critical evaluations for moving image work.

OCR Media Studies A2 – 2734 Critical Research Study
The case study on Lynne Ramsay would be appropriate for the Women and Film topic; the *Alien* case study is appropriate for the Concept to Product topic, as is the material on the Hollywood studio system.

OCR Media Studies A2 – 2735 Media Issues and Debates
The whole guide, but particularly the sections on genre and authorship are relevant to the topic, The Concept of Genre in Film; the case study on Lynne Ramsay is relevant to the topic, British Cinema since 1990.

WJEC Media Studies A2 – ME4: Investigating Media Texts
Any students choosing to do coursework research on film will benefit from a sense of the problems of authorship and the co-operative nature of filmmaking.

WJEC Media Studies A2 – ME5: Changing Media Industries

The Lynne Ramsay case study is relevant to the topic element Contemporary British Film. The genre section and the case study on romantic comedy are useful when preparing the Cinema Audiences element.

WJEC Film Studies AS – FS1, FS2, FS3

While this guide is more directly relevant to the A2 portion of the specification, we feel the idea of the auteur can and should be introduced during the AS course, since this encourages students to see the films studied as art as well as entertainment product. The case study on Lynne Ramsay in particular is useful preparation for the micro analysis and will fit into a scheme of work for the Scottish Cinema option. The FS3 text *Brief Encounter* has accordingly been used as a centrepiece for a resource on shared authorship.

WJEC Film Studies – A2 FS4: Making Meaning 2

There is an obvious element of preparation for the individual auteur study here. Additionally, students who choose the Film Journalism option may wish to contrast their pieces by adopting an auteur-based style in one and another perspective (such as genre) in the second. Students who choose filmmaking will become low-budget auteurs themselves, while those who choose scriptwriting will emphasise either an auteurist or industry-based approach. A solid grasp of the debates will make for more convincing work and more confident evaluation.

WJEC Film Studies – A2 FS5: Studies in World Cinema

The issue of authorship in non-Hollywood contexts is introduced in Section 2. The notion of the auteur is particularly relevant to the New Waves topic, but can be applied throughout the study of texts for this paper.

WJEC Film Studies – A2 FS6: Critical Studies

There is obvious relevance to the topic: Genre and Authorship Studies. Additionally, the case study on Dustin Hoffman, as well as elements of the *Alien* case study and portions of Section 2 concerning shared authorship will help prepare students for the topic: Performance Studies.

Other parts of this guide can enhance students' understanding of the FS6 topics: Fandom – and Its Significance to the Film Industry; Independent Film and Its Audience; The Dominance of Hollywood and Indigenous Film Production; Shocking Cinema.

CCEA Moving Image Arts AS – Unit 3: Film Fiction

The guide as a whole offers pertinent background and teaching ideas for this unit. Much of the material is directed towards audience attitudes to film authorship, and understanding the role of the director. There is discussion of film genre in relation to gangster and romantic comedy films. The *Alien* case study is particularly useful when teaching pre-production. (At the time of writing, the A2 specification for this qualification has not been published.)

SQA Media Studies Higher – Unit DF14 12 Media Analysis: Fiction
Auteur, stars and genre are defined by this specification as categories for analysis of media texts: all three of these elements are addressed throughout the guide. The case study on Lynne Ramsay creates opportunities for discussing authorship and representation in a Scottish context.

SQA Media Studies Advanced Higher – Unit D332 13 Media Analysis
The Advanced Higher Media Analysis unit requires candidates to apply and evaluate an analytical approach that has been important in the interpretation of a particular medium. Auteur theory is an excellent model of such an approach. This guide provides a thorough evaluation of the auteur-critical approach.

SQA Media Studies Advanced Higher – Unit D37A 13 Media Investigation
Critical assessment of auteur theory is identified as a significant potential issue for this unit.

Why auteur study?

(NB: The question, Who or what is an auteur? is addressed in Section 2, pp16.)

In some cases, for example, for those who are delivering A2 Level Film Studies in the UK, auteur study is a compulsory element of the specification. However, there are good reasons why every course involving study of film should take the auteur approach into account. This is an important tradition in Film Studies, and, arguably, it was only because of the auteur theory that academics began to take Hollywood cinema seriously as an art form. Directors, many of whom have seen themselves as auteurs, have rewritten the language of cinema throughout its history.

The issue of auteur study also draws in ideas about creative control, particularly when we start looking at the idea that an auteur does not necessarily have to be a director. Whatever we think film is, it is a creative art, and auteurist approaches are about looking for the sources of creation and art in the filmmaking process. In other words, to grasp the debate about authorship, students need to grasp the processes of filmmaking: what do an editor, a cinematographer and a screenwriter actually do? Consequently it is as relevant to a study of the industry as it is to a study of film as art.

From an audience point of view, the experience of film has frequently been based on the persona of an auteur. Why else call a movie 'Alfred Hitchcock's *Rope*' or 'the fourth film by Quentin Tarantino'? Through a critical grasp of the idea of authorship, students can grow to a more sophisticated understanding of their own behaviour as viewers.

How to use this guide

We have based the structure of the pack on our experience of delivering Media Studies and Film Studies at AS and A Level to adolescent and adult students. The films we have selected as examples are all ones we have found to be 'student-friendly', either because students already know them or because they have been positively received in the classroom. There is a bias towards popular US film here, but we have also included reference to many less mainstream films.

Throughout the writing process, we have aimed for three learning outcomes:
1. Developing a knowledge of the main auteur theories and theorists.
2. Putting auteur criticism in the context of real filmmakers, their films and the film industry.
3. Applying these to students' own auteur studies, theoretical essays and to reflections on their own creative work.

We expect teachers to use the guide in three ways:
1. To build up a confident basic knowledge of auteur theory and the debates surrounding it.
2. To obtain ready-to-use activities, advice and resources for classroom use.
3. To provide structures and schemes of work, building in sequence.

For teachers new to auteur theory and/or to film study in general, the fullest benefit will be achieved from working through the whole text sequentially, particularly Section 2. Others may choose to dip in to individual activities and subsections.

The classroom resources offer a range of materials and are all related directly to issues raised in this guide.
- Some present students with activities.
- Some support the viewing of films, key extracts or documentary material.
- Some provide models of writing from an auteur-based or alternative perspective.

To access the pages, when asked, enter username: **auteur** and the password: **te2103au**. If you have any problems, email: education.resources@bfi.org.uk

Section 2 divides into two major subsections:
- An introduction to the history of auteur criticism, aimed at teachers who have little or no previous knowledge of this area.
- An exploration of various ways that auteur-based approaches can be applied to Hollywood and world cinemas.

This is not by any means a definitive account; it is an outline of auteur criticism, which will give the teacher confidence to discuss these concepts with classes working at UK secondary advanced level or its equivalent. Wherever possible, we have therefore indicated further reading for those who wish to develop their understanding of a particular strand.

Section 3 takes the ideas from Section 2 and expands on them through four case studies. The first two of these explore issues in a way that will prepare students to produce more theoretically-based essays, but also to provide ideas that will be relevant when working on their own Auteur Studies.

Case studies 3 and 4 give examples of individual auteur studies, but similarly can operate as preparation for more theoretical work. For example, the study on Lynne Ramsay would fit into the WJEC Film Studies specification as an example of a coursework Auteur Study (FS4), an example of Scottish Cinema (FS3), an example of micro or macro analysis (FS1), and a springboard for creative film production (FS4). It can also be used to illustrate elements of the A2 OCR, AQA and WJEC Media Studies specifications.

Getting started

Introducing students to the idea of authorship is generally best achieved through exploring their own experiences as audiences.

The idea of authorship has long been an important one in the industry. In the early days of cinema, D W Griffith would place his name prominently in his work and in publicity material because his authorship was recognised as a guarantee of quality. Later, Chaplin, Ford, Huston and Hitchcock took similar approaches, and the names of Spielberg, Scott and Cameron are used in the same way by present-day Hollywood. Audiences see such names as synonymous with 'quality', and this reaction is encouraged by studios as another tool, along with genre and star power, for the selling of films.

To put an individual name and/or face to the film seems to fulfil a basic human desire: the need to personalise. However, for audiences, the author is by no means always the director. In fact, popular assessments of a film's authorship often seem to depend on the type of film it is.

● Activity

A useful starting activity is to ask students to track down original reviews of *The Lord of the Rings: The Fellowship of the Ring* (Peter Jackson, USA, 2001) on the internet, beginning with Philip French's review for the *Observer* (16 December, 2001) at: http://film.guardian.co.uk/News_Story/Critic_Review/Observer_Film_of_the_week/0,4267,619446,00.html.

They will find a strong sense of authorship; but it is Tolkien, the writer of the novel on which the film was based, who takes priority. There are a number of reasons for this, which include the following:

- Peter Jackson was not an especially well-known director at that time.
- *The Lord of the Rings* was not a 'natural next step' for Jackson, based on his previous work.
- The cost and scale of the production were enormous, making the director seem insignificant.
- The story, setting and characters were already very well known, so that for much of the audience, the key question was 'will this film be authentic to Tolkien?'

The source of the original material has a strong impact on the way audiences identify authors, or have them identified through marketing. With adaptations, audiences are often divided between the film's personnel and the original writer, depending on whether or not they already know the book. In 1972, a new film by, at that time almost unknown, Francis Ford Coppola, giving Al Pacino his debut film role, had to be titled *Mario Puzo's The Godfather* after the writer of the novel it was based upon (and co-writer of the screenplay). These days, Coppola and Pacino are the figures most strongly associated with the film; but for cinema audiences in 1972, Puzo was the author. Considering that example, it is possible that in time, Jackson will become for most audiences the author of *The Lord of the Rings* film trilogy.

To emphasise the point that different audiences will focus on different author figures, an excellent example is *The Shining* (Stanley Kubrick, USA, 1980).

- This film is (fairly loosely) based on a novel by Stephen King, the most successful horror writer in the world.
- It was directed by Stanley Kubrick, who had already established himself as an auteur director.
- It starred Jack Nicholson, a major Hollywood actor with an intensely personal performing style.

Each of these major contributors had very high status among a section of the film's potential audience. Thus, for different sections of the audience, the film will have 'belonged to' or been 'by' each of those figures. King has subsequently given his name to a TV miniseries version, *Stephen King's The Shining* (Mick Garris, USA, 1997) which is certainly truer to his novel. Effectively this action withdrew King's authorship from the Kubrick version. Audiences who are most strongly interested in seeing an 'authentic' adaptation are strongly supportive of this version; while those who value film for itself tend to favour the version made by Kubrick in 1980. Students can research this author battle for themselves by looking at the 'user comments' section for the film and the TV versions of *The Shining* at www.imdb.com.

Another important element is the type of film. For lovers of independent and semi-independent filmmaking, directorial authorship is a key issue. A search for reviews of films by Jim Jarmusch will produce statements of this type:

The effect Jarmusch achieves is so enjoyable and distinctive, and it shows something individually and engagingly developed in its approach … (Review of *Ghost Dog: The Way of the Samurai* by Peter Bradshaw, *The Guardian* 2000)

A good beginning, therefore, is to ask students to consider which films, if any, have led them to an interest in the director, as opposed to the stars or the genre. This will prepare them for the basic principles of traditional 'auteur theory'.

Scheme of work 1: Introducing auteur study

Time: Six weeks (ideally five hours per week)

Aims:
On completing this unit students should be able to:
- Understand the key concepts of auteur theory.
- Apply these concepts to Lynne Ramsay and Dustin Hoffman.
- Develop the research and evaluation skills needed for auteur study.

Outcomes:
- Preparation for students' individual auteur research projects.
- Collection of case study material for WJEC exam questions on Authorship and Genre and Performance Studies on the Critical Studies paper.

(NB The worksheets and student notes indicated in bold can be found at www.bfi.org.uk/tfms. To access these resources enter username: **auteur**, password: **te2103au**.)

Week 1   Discuss 'the artist'
Worksheet 2
Introduce and debate definitions
Worksheet 1
Present Sarris's 'circles'
Screen *Small Deaths, Kill the Day* and *Gasman* and analyse Lynne Ramsay's individual style
Student notes (on Lynne Ramsay, Case study 3)

Week 2   Lynne Ramsay as auteur
Screen *Ratcatcher*
Analyse Lynne Ramsay's key themes
Worksheet 16 and **Student notes**
Discuss authorship in *Morvern Callar*
Debate: Ramsay as auteur vs Ramsay as social realist
Worksheet 17 and **Student notes**
Essay: Does Ramsay's individual style interfere with the social message of *Ratcatcher*?

Week 3 Dustin Hoffman: actor–auteur

See teaching notes for Case study 4

Compare the 'auteur' and the 'actor–auteur'

Analyse the conflict between actor and director; scene analysis of *The Graduate* and *Tootsie*

Present the Star System, including key terms such as 'typecasting' and 'range'

Analyse scenes from *Midnight Cowboy, Tootsie* and *Rain Man*

Student notes: Dustin Hoffman: Analysis of character and performance

Discuss Hoffman's position in the Star System

Week 4 Creative control and Method acting

Introduce of the idea of creative control

Worksheet 18

Screen the rest of *Tootsie*

Present Method acting; mini research task

Worksheet 19

Weeks 5 and **6** Auteur research projects

Students plan auteur research projects

Worksheets 20 and **21**

Students begin auteur research projects

Scheme of work 2: Authorship and genre

Time: Six weeks (may take longer, depending on arrangements for screening – ideally five hours per week)

Prior knowledge:
- Basic grasp of the Hollywood studio system;
- Basic grasp of auteur theory.

Aims:

On completing this unit students should be able to:
- Through practical application of their knowledge to two different genres, one 'serious' and one 'comic', compare an accepted auteur against a figure whose work is less highly regarded.
- Explore the ways in which our ideas of authorship, value and the classics of the future are often dependent on accepted values.

Outcomes:
- Understanding that P J Hogan's three films are fresh, imaginative and groundbreaking, especially compared to flat, formulaic genre work like *Picture Perfect*.

- Assessment of why he is less well regarded than directors like Coppola, even though both directors – in these examples – are making new versions of old genres.

(NB The worksheets and student notes indicated in bold can be found at www.bfi.org.uk/tfms. To access these resources enter username: **auteur**, password: **te2103au**.)

Week 1   What is genre?
Students share experiences of genre: What genres do they enjoy? How do they use genre to select films to view? How is genre used in the promotion of films? What sorts of cinema are less likely to use genre?
View a range of trailers and posters to identify the importance of genre in constructing and promoting Hollywood film
Screen *Angels with Dirty Faces.* Discuss what makes this a typical gangster genre film. Which elements now seem clichéd and stereotypical?
Homework: Research Warner Brothers gangster films of this period What were their shared characteristics?

Week 2   Genre or auteur?
Screen *The Godfather*
Students do semi-independent research (using the library and internet) into Francis Ford Coppola's career as a director
Compare the endings of *The Godfather* and *Angels with Dirty Faces*
Worksheet 6
Worksheet 7

Week 3   Genre or auteur presentations
In small groups, students prepare short presentations based on chosen sequences from *The Godfather* and *Angels with Dirty Faces* to support the argument that Coppola is an auteur and Curtiz is not
Deliver presentations

Week 4   Romantic comedy
Use key extracts from *Picture Perfect* to identify key features of the romcom genre
Student notes on *Picture Perfect*
Worksheets 13 and **14**
Screen *Muriel's Wedding*
Discuss: Is *Muriel's Wedding* a romcom? What sort of film would we expect Hogan to make next?

Homework: Read Andy Medhurst's article in *Sight and Sound* on *Muriel's Wedding* at http://www.bfi.org.uk/sightandsound/2002_07/feature02_ButImBeautiful.html

Week 5 *My Best Friend's Wedding*
Outline Hogan's career
Discuss why Hollywood likes genre
Screen *My Best Friend's Wedding*
Worksheet 15
Homework: List the similarities and differences between the films

Week 6 *Unconditional Love*
Introduce: This is the film Hogan used all his Hollywood auteur power to make
Screen *Unconditional Love*
Ask for students' immediate responses
Discuss: Were New Line right to deny it a cinema release?
If a 'serious' film like *The Godfather* is an auteur work, can a whimsical piece like *Unconditional Love* be an auteur film too?
Essay: Which is more useful as a means of analysing Hogan's films: a genre approach or auteurism?

2

Background

Definitions

What is auteur theory? And, more to the point, who or what is an auteur? As with any theory, the arguments surrounding authorship rest on its definitions, so it is useful for students to be exposed to these from the beginning and to form their own responses to them, as they will become relevant later on. Literally, auteur is French for 'author' and in Film Studies refers to one or more of the following:

- The principal creator of a film;
- The principal source of meaning in a film;
- A filmmaker who demonstrates technical excellence;
- A filmmaker who makes films of artistic merit as opposed to commercial value;
- A filmmaker who makes films with an individual style;
- A filmmaker who makes films with similar themes;
- A filmmaker who adopts a 'jack of all trades' approach to film-making;
- A group of filmmakers who make a 'great' film.

Simply put, auteur theory asks the question: which of these definitions is true? Many pages in many film journals and books have been filled with attempts to answer this question; here we attempt to answer it in only a few. A more in-depth discussion of auteur theory can be found in *The Cinema Book* (Cook and Bernink, 1999) and extracts from key theoretical texts can be found in *Theories of Authorship: A Reader* (Caughie, 1981). The important questions to ask when considering auteur theory are:

- Who is the author of a film? Is it the writer, the producer, the director, the actor? Or, since film is a collaborative art, shouldn't we attribute authorship to a group of people?
- Which criteria should we use to define an author? Creative control? Technical mastery? Artistic merit? Individual style? Thematic consistency?

- What limitations are imposed on the auteur? Financial pressures? Genre conventions? Tradition?
- Finally, does studying an auteur enhance or limit our understanding of a film? For instance, which aspects of a film are excluded from our analysis – social and historical context, individual interpretation, and so on?

Worksheet 1 Auteur theory: Definitions

Use this worksheet to raise the above questions with a class. To explore these questions in full, however, it is important to understand the history of auteur theory from its origins in Romanticism through to the critical theory of Roland Barthes.

To access worksheets and other online materials go to **www.bfi.org.uk/tfms** and enter User name: **auteur** and Password: **te2103au**.

Romanticism

The idea of art being a form of individual expression comes from Romanticism (1780–1848). In this period, art was seen as being characterised by:

Art	Artist
originality	originator
individual expression	individual
emotion	sensitive
imagination	dreamer or visionary
political radicalism	outsider/political radical

This shift towards individualism can be accounted for in a number of ways. Two of them are relevant to our discussion of authorship.

First, Romanticism was a reaction to the Augustan Age when artists used classical models for their art. The Romantics believed art should be original and focused on the individual self as a source of inspiration, using their own experience or imagination as a starting point for expression. We can see parallels with the auteur working in Hollywood. The film theorist, André Bazin, for example, has described American cinema as a 'classical art' (Caughie, 1981, pp45–46). The studio system developed its own set of rules and models that defined films during this period. Artists working within this system may have felt these limited their creativity.

Second, the Romantic period saw changes in the distribution and exhibition of art, which in turn altered the relationship between the artist and his/her audience. The invention of the printing press and the introduction of the art gallery meant writers and painters were freed from the authority of their patron, but became dependent on a new, middle-class public with an increasing appetite for novels, poetry and painting. Art became subject to economic forces; the dilemma for the artist was more obviously between artistic integrity and pleasing the public. Here further parallels with Hollywood can be seen. 'Show business' is one that prioritises 'entertainment' over 'art' – a distinction emphasised by auteurist critics. Consequently, the true 'artists' of Hollywood are often perceived as working outside the system and are associated with independent production companies or low-budget films.

Worksheet 2 Auteur theory: The artist

The Romantic conception of the artist can be introduced to the students using Caspar David Friedrich's painting, *Wanderer above the Sea of Fog* (1818). Friedrich's depiction of the romantic hero as an isolated visionary inspired by Nature is a useful starting point for discussion.

To access worksheets and other online materials go to **www.bfi.org.uk/tfms** and enter User name: **auteur** and Password: **te2103au**.

worksheet ② Auteur theory: The artist

Caspar David Friedrich (1774–1840), Wanderer above the Mists (c.1818), oil on canvas, 94.8 x 74.8 cm, Kunsthalle, Hamburg

Activity

1 How is the man in this painting portrayed?
2 Name five famous artists and five famous film directors.
3 In your view, what qualities should an artist possess?
4 In your view, what qualities should a film director possess?
5 Are they the same or different?
6 Where do we get these ideas from?

Page 1 of 1   Auteur Study

Cahiers du Cinéma:
François Truffaut and André Bazin

To introduce *Cahiers du Cinéma* see **Worksheet 3 Auteur theory: Film as art?**

Only late in the history of cinema was film taken seriously as an art form because:

- From the Lumières to the special effects movie, it has traditionally been regarded as an 'amusement';
- It is made by a group, not an individual;
- It is dependent on technology;
- It is dependent on money;
- It is reproduced in countless cinemas, as well as on TV, video, DVD and the internet;
- It appeals to a mass audience.

To access worksheets and other online materials go to **www.bfi.org.uk/tfms** and enter User name: **auteur** and Password: **te2103au**.

1 of 2 pages

Disagreement remains as to whether the critics who first proposed the idea of the auteur in the French film journal, *Cahiers du Cinéma*, in the 1950s were attempting to liberate the director from the restrictions of the system or to redefine film as a serious, if not elitist, art form. They did not speak as one however. The journal was a focal point for many voices, the strongest of which were those of the critic (and later director), François Truffaut, and the film theorist, André Bazin.

In his famous 1954 essay, 'Une certaine tendance du cinéma français', Truffaut attacked 'la tradition de la qualité' dominating French cinema at the time, which saw the writer as central to the creative process, with the majority of screenplays adapted from literary novels. Opposing this tradition, Truffaut emphasised *mise en scène*, or the visual qualities of a film, in order to portray the director as the principal creative force. He also made a key distinction between the auteur, a director with his or her own visual style, and the *metteur en scène* – a director who simply translated a screenplay into a film. His article was essentially polemical and his aim was to champion a cinema that utilised these cinematic qualities and to promote the role of the director in an environment where s/he was undervalued. It is no coincidence that Truffaut, along with the other members of the *nouvelle vague* or French New Wave (Godard, Chabrol, Rohmer, Rivette, etc), went on to make his own innovative films.

André Bazin is often seen as a father figure to Truffaut, the *Cahiers* critics and the directors of *nouvelle vague*, so it is perhaps surprising that he argued against *la politique des auteurs*. Bazin believed in the potential for cinema to record a social or historical reality. According to Bazin, a director should not impose his or her own personal vision onto the film through the manipulation of *mise en scène*. Instead, ambient lighting, deep focus, and the long take should focus the viewer's attention on the reality of what was being filmed. By way of example, he preferred the Italian neo-realists to the German Expressionists. In his 1957 essay, 'La Politique des auteurs', Bazin criticised:

- The idea that the worst work of an auteur is better than the best work of a *metteur en scène*;
- The fact that social and historical aspects are passed over in favour of personal signatures;
- The negation of the film in favour of the auteur: '*Auteur*, yes, but what *of*?' (Caughie, 1981, p46).

Auteur theory: *Movie* magazine and Andrew Sarris

In Britain, there was a similar undertaking in the pages of *Movie* magazine. In his 1962 essay, 'Films, directors, and critics', one of the editors, Ian Cameron, set out their agenda:

> On the whole, we accept this cinema of directors, although without going to the farthest of extremes of la politique des auteurs.

Like *Cahiers,* the *Movie* position was largely based on disaffection with the climate of British film at the time, dominated as it was by social realism and lacking any directors with individual style and vision, but Cameron was keen to emphasise their differences from the *Cahiers* position:

- Cameron felt the auteur approach was important, but did not believe the director's word was final:

> When the director disagrees with the critics this does not mean the critics are wrong, for, after all, the value of a film depends on the film itself, and not on the director's intentions, which may not be apparent from the finished work.

This criticism echoes Bazin.

- Again echoing Bazin, he also disagreed with the evaluative distinction between auteur and *metteur en scène*,

  > which makes it difficult to think of a bad director making a good film and almost impossible to think of a good director making a bad one.

- Criticising the rigidity of *la politique des auteurs*, Cameron argues that the director was not the only person who qualified as the author of a film. He identifies other candidates: the writer, the photographer, the composer, the producer, and the star. In addition, he suggests authorship can be located in 'magnificent collaborators', citing *Casablanca* (Michael Curtiz, USA, 1942) as an example.

- Finally, he suggests other ways of looking at a film: how the iconography of a film reflects the society in which it was made, or else 'the picture of the audience' a film provides.

With all these qualifiers it is perhaps important to stress the fact that Cameron felt

> [t]he assumption which underlies all the writing in *Movie* is that the director is the author of the film, the person who gives it any distinctive quality it may have. (Caughie, 1981, pp51–55).

In America, the critic Andrew Sarris was the key figure in adopting the auteur approach, in his essay 'Notes on the Auteur Theory in 1962' and later in *The American Cinema: Directors and Directions, 1929–68*. He wanted Hollywood films to be taken seriously in a critical environment that was both dismissive and condescending. His list of 'pantheon directors', including John Ford, D W Griffith, Howard Hawks and Orson Welles, were evaluated according to three premises or 'circles':

> [T]he first premise of the auteur theory is the technical competence of the director as a criterion of value…

Consequently, a technically incompetent director (Ed Wood, for example) is 'automatically cast out of the pantheon of directors'.

> The second premise of the auteur theory is the distinguishable personality of the director as criterion of value. Over a group of films, a director must exhibit certain recurring characteristics of style, which serve as a signature. The way a film looks and moves should have some relationship to the way a director thinks and feels.
> …
> The third and ultimate premise of the auteur theory is concerned with interior meaning, the ultimate glory of the cinema as art. Interior meaning is extrapolated from the tension between a director's personality and his material, but also the demands of a star or the pressures imposed by a producer. (Caughie, 1981, pp63–4)

Sarris's approach was highly influential, but soon came under attack, most notably from the critic Pauline Kael, who, in her 1963 essay 'Circles and Squares', argued

> auteur theory is an attempt by adult males to justify staying inside the small range of experience of their boyhood and adolescence. (Cited in Gerstner and Staiger, 2003, p9)

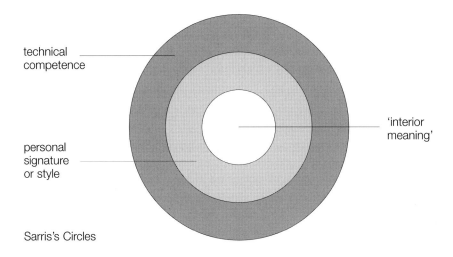

technical competence

personal signature or style

'interior meaning'

Sarris's Circles

The influence of critical theory

Finally, it is important to note the influence of critical theory on auteurism, in particular, the cultural anthropologist, Claude Lévi-Strauss, and the critical theorist, Roland Barthes.

● Claude Lévi-Strauss

Although Levi-Strauss was not a film critic himself, the method he used to analyse myths in different cultures was appropriated by film critics as an approach to auteur study. This approach, known as structuralism, attempted to identify the underlying structure in a story as opposed to focusing on content or style. Critics such as Geoffrey Nowell-Smith, Peter Wollen and Charles Eckert employed this method when looking at an individual director. In his seminal study *Signs and Meaning in the Cinema*, for example, Wollen explains:

> [B]y a process of comparison with other films, it is possible to decipher, not a coherent message or world-view, but a structure which underlies the film and shapes it, gives it a certain pattern of energy cathexis. It is this structure which auteur analysis disengages from the film. (Caughie (ed), 1981, p146)

For the auteur–structuralist, these underlying structures took the form of 'oppositions' in the text. Wollen, for example, found the following oppositions in the films of John Ford:

- East versus West
- Garden versus wilderness
- Civilised versus savage
- Married versus unmarried
- Book versus gun.

These oppositions were thought by Wollen to define Ford's body of work, but he also went on to identify differences and variations within individual films.

Inevitably, however, auteur–structuralism was criticised, in this case by Robin Wood and Brian Henderson who argued it was reductionist, but more succinctly through the reservations of one its own proponents, Nowell-Smith, in his original essay on Visconti. According to Nowell-Smith, the structuralist approach ignored:

- 'The possibility of an author's work changing through time';
- The possibility of 'the structures being variable and not constant';
and finally
- 'non-thematic subject-matter and sub-stylistic features of the visual treatment'. (Caughie, 1981, p137).

Go to www.bfi.org.uk/tfms for an approach to **exploring auteur–structuralism**. (Username: **auteur** Password: **te2103au**)

● Roland Barthes

The second theorist relevant to our survey of authorship is Roland Barthes. The French critic was known primarily for his work on semiotics and, in particular, his influential essay, 'The Death of the Author' (1968), the key points of which are summarised below:

- Critics who use the author as the criterion of meaning of a film do so as a means of winning a critical debate. As Barthes writes, 'when the author has been found, the text is "explained" – victory to the critic'. They are just as concerned with their own authority as a critic as they are in understanding the film.
- It is the reader, not the writer, who 'completes' the meaning of a text: 'a text's unity lies not in its origin but in its destination'.
- Finally, language is described by Barthes as 'a tissue of quotations'. The writer cannot be original; s/he only has the power to 'mix writings'. In the case of film language, it is impossible to attribute authorship to an individual director as s/he can only recycle formula and convention.

Barthes concludes his essay by proclaiming that 'the birth of the reader must be at the cost of the death of the Author' (Caughie, 1981, p211–13).

'**The death of the author**' is a difficult idea for students to get to grips with. The activities described in the online notes at www.bfi.org.uk/tfms attempt to illustrate the role of the critic and the role of the reader respectively.

Issues in film authorship

It is important to develop students' knowledge of auteur theory and its history, as previously detailed. However, most teachers will find that the real point of interest for students will be in exploring the relevance of these concepts to the study of film and the practice of filmmaking.

Often the usefulness of the auteur approach is revealed through comparison or conflict with other ways of defining films. For example, in the Auteur Study required for second-year coursework (FS4) by A Level Film Studies, students are expected to approach their chosen auteur through a 'problematic' such as the co-operative nature of most filmmaking. In Media Studies, the reverse is common. Here the main focus is genre and the film industry. While art cinema and independent film will be more relevant to Film Studies, the starting point for both subjects is the mainstream industry. There is some overlap between Media and Film Studies in discussion of popular texts like *Psycho* (Alfred Hitchcock, USA, 1960) or *Alien* (Ridley Scott, USA, 1979).

● 1. Authorship versus auteurship

The definition of authorship seems to be widening, so that auteur study can be carried out on a variety of filmmaking artists, and not only on directors. This moves the definition of auteur away from Sarris and the *Cahiers* critics and even takes it further than Ian Cameron. To clarify students' understanding, it helps to distinguish between 'authorship' and 'auteurship', retaining some of the spirit of Sarris's 'circles' but dropping the attachment to directors alone. Accordingly:

● Authorship is concerned with who 'owns' the film as a whole, who is its author.
● Auteurship is concerned with artistic intent and realisation.
● Authors and auteurs can be anyone who makes a significant creative contribution to the film.

This means that a director can be an author or an auteur, but so can a studio, a star or a cinematographer. It also means that authorship and auteurship may be shared. This eliminates many of the problems inherent in the proposals of

Truffaut and Sarris. However, it needs to be made clear to students that it is an alternative perspective and that it contradicts the basic ideal of classical auteurism, which is the director as a single, uncontestable auteur.

● 2. Authorship and auteurship in Hollywood

Before you start discussing the idea of 'Hollywood auteurs' remind your class about the range of contexts in which film is – and has been – produced. Keep things simple, since all you want to do is provide some context for the idea of authorship. We suggest that you identify and explain the basic differences between the following three types of film production:

- Commercial/industrial film production (eg Hollywood, Bollywood);
- State-funded/subsidised film production (eg UK Film Council);
- Independent and/or smaller-scale producers with an arts or auteurist agenda (in Europe, eg FilmFour, Studio Canal; in America, eg Miramax).

The following historical summary should be adequate to your needs, but for a more detailed introduction to Hollywood, we recommend the section 'Cinema as Institution' in *An Introduction to Film Studies* (Nelmes, 2003).

When discussing Hollywood auteurs, the core issue is almost always the tension between the creative individual and the 'machine'. Crudely, there are three main 'periods' of authorship in Hollywood:

- The vertically integrated studio system (1930–1950);
- The age of auteur freedom (late 1960s–1970s)
- High-concept and independent Hollywood (1980s on)

The vertically integrated studio system (1930–1950)

It is hard to imagine conditions less likely to produce auteur directors than those of the Hollywood studio system. Directors were contracted to be on-set managers, turning out genre films to tight deadlines and strict budgets. Everything was watched over by the producers, to prevent excessively costly or 'artistic' decisions. As Bordwell and Thompson explain (2004, pp310–33), all filmmakers had to conform to the 'continuity rules' regarding editing and camerawork. And yet, despite these restrictions on artistic freedom, the system produced a large number of distinctive and creative films.

Partly, this was due to directors struggling for more creative control. Looking back on the studio era, the *Cahiers* critics recognised that pure authorship in Hollywood was an ideal. However they found that some directors had used the studio system in the way that a painter would use a brush or a writer a pen. Successful, proven directors were given greater control over their own work. John Ford was allowed this privilege and this is one of the reasons Sarris and others see him as an auteur. Alternatively, if the biography of the director contains evidence of battles fought by directors against producers, this is often taken as proof of auteur power. The most famous instance of this is Alfred Hitchcock versus David O Selznick.

The *Cahiers du Cinéma* critics argued that the 'great films' could only have been made because auteurs were at work within the system. This is Truffaut's idea that there are no good or bad films, only good or bad directors. However, there are alternative perspectives.

Were the Hollywood studios auteurs in their own right?

As we have already suggested, an auteur does not have to be a single artist. It is possible to see particular studios in this period as being auteurs. Each had its own recognisable house style, based on repeated genre and themes as well as formal elements such as sets, film stock, lighting and casting. For example, the Warner Brothers 'social issues' films of the 1930s and 40s, such as *Angels with Dirty Faces* (Michael Curtiz, USA, 1938) and *They Drive by Night* (Raoul Walsh, USA, 1940), tended to have a leftist bias, portrayed contemporary working-class lifestyles, were all shot in monochrome and repeatedly used the same group of (contracted) actors. This kind of repetition may be seen as the auteur signature of the studio.

The recognisable characteristics of each of the eight studios during the studio system years make them excellent subjects for auteur study. However, students should also consider the question of quality. The first priority of Hollywood was not art, and the studios were indifferent to aesthetic quality as long as the movies were profitable. For that reason, they may be better described as 'authors' rather than as 'auteurs'.

Were the 'classic movies' all directed by auteurs?

Most of the generic movies made by the studio system are now long forgotten. The films now seen as 'classics' of the period are quite a small proportion of the whole. Discuss with students to what extent history supports Truffaut's idea that there are no good and bad movies, only good and bad directors. Why do some films end up as classics while others are forgotten? In literature, the classics can be defined as the works of the great authors. Do we find similar conditions apply in the cinema of the Hollywood studio era? Three key questions to be discussed are:

1. Who decides what is a classic?
2. Were the forgotten movies of this period actually 'no good'?
3. Why are the so-called 'classics' regarded so highly?

The process by which Hollywood films end up in the 'classics' list is complex, but we would expect to find some or all of the following characteristics:

- The film is the work of an 'auteur' or 'great' director;
- The film has been identified as 'good' in some way;

- The film is seen as being sociologically important;
- The film includes a performance by an important star or stars;
- The film represents an important technical or aesthetic development in cinema;
- The film represents an important development in cinematic subject matter;
- The film still has an audience.

Citizen Kane (Orson Welles, USA, 1941) has all seven of these. *The Wizard of Oz* (Victor Fleming, USA, 1939) has most of them (perhaps all, since an uncredited King Vidor shot the Kansas sequences). Even the remarkably bad independent production *Plan 9 from Outer Space* (Edward D Wood Jr, USA, 1959) has one, and perhaps the most important, of these characteristics: it still has an audience.

It is interesting to identify the 'quality' films produced by a studio within this period and see if there were common 'team' elements in their making. Searching the big studio names of this period on www.imdb.com produces enormous lists of films, most of which are forgotten. The famous ones tend to be the work of well-known directors, including some who are considered Hollywood auteurs: Howard Hawks, King Vidor, Michael Curtiz, Fritz Lang, Cecil B DeMille, John Huston, Alfred Hitchcock and so on. From a Truffaut/Sarris auteurist point of view, this would be taken as evidence for their view of Hollywood. Here is proof that auteurs fought within the Hollywood machine to create groundbreaking, artistically valid work, while all around them, the *metteurs en scène* were churning out generic entertainment product. It does seem that there is some truth in this view.

Alternatively, you could argue against the auteurist account of Hollywood as follows:

- Sarris and other auteurist critics have created a canon of so-called 'greatest films' and 'greatest directors' based on their own tastes and prejudices.
- Films and directors that did not end up on these critics' lists have been ignored.
- The ignored films might be just as good as, or even better than, the films included in the canon – they have been ignored because they did not fit the auteurist plan.
- The films in the canon continue to be reproduced on DVD and VHS, and to be shown in specialist cinemas; the films outside the canon are mostly unavailable to audiences.

In other words, one possible interpretation of the influence of auteur theory, and Sarris in particular, would say that it has distorted our understanding of studio system Hollywood in favour of a narrow range of directors. The result has been undeserved oblivion for hundreds of movies from this period.

27

This is worth discussing, and there is possibly some truth in it too. However, it is not completely convincing either, for two reasons:

1. Many 'classic movies' were the work of directors who did not fit the auteur criteria. Fred Zinnemann, the director of *High Noon* (USA, 1959), was dismissed by Sarris as 'superficial'; John Huston's body of work contains a large number of movie greats, but is so inconsistent in style and subject that he cannot be said to have defined a 'signature'.

2. A great deal of very minor Hollywood product is actually still available for anyone who wants to see it. In recent years, video, DVD, cable and digital TV have increased our access to these movies.

Worksheet 4 Investigating a minor director from the Hollywood Studio era (c1930–1948)

This worksheet helps students to explore the notion of major and minor directors. It also encourages thinking about the interaction between critical opinion and audience interest in the formation of 'classic' status for films and auteur status for their directors.

To access worksheets and other online materials go to **www.bfi.org.uk/tfms** and enter User name: **auteur** and Password: **te2103au**.

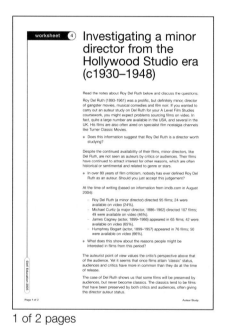

1 of 2 pages

The age of auteur freedom (late 1960s–70s)

We can see the 15–20 year period after the breaking up of the studio system at the end of the 1940s as a time of transition. Some interesting experiments in authorship took place during this period. For example, the actor Burt Lancaster used his new-found power to set up his own production company (Hecht-Hill-Lancaster) and famously alternated between crowd pleasing money-makers like *The Crimson Pirate* (Robert Siodmak, USA, 1952) or *Airport* (George Seaton, USA, 1970) and more personal, esoteric projects like *Birdman of Alcatraz* (John Frankenheimer, USA, 1962) and *The Swimmer* (Frank Perry, USA,1968).

Andrew Sarris's criticism in *Village Voice*, along with the publication of *The American Cinema: Directors and Directions 1929–1968,* seems to have had a powerful effect on the way people in Hollywood thought about movies. Sarris's influence, together with the success of unconventional films created by maverick directors, such as *Bonnie and Clyde* (Arthur Penn, USA, 1967), led to a period of about 10 years in which Hollywood looked for, and rewarded, those it saw as auteurs. The consequence was a succession of highly regarded big-budget films made with the intention of satisfying an individual vision rather than playing to audience expectations. Among the most accessible and entertaining accounts of this period is Peter Biskind's book, *Easy Riders, Raging Bulls* (1999) and the documentary based on it. Biskind takes the line that this was the one period in Hollywood when directors were genuinely allowed to be auteurs, and that they abused this freedom so badly that it was finally taken away from them.

Whereas the directors of the studio age had been defined as auteurs after developing their careers, Biskind shows how film-school graduates like Coppola and Lucas set out from the beginning with the intention of becoming Hollywood auteurs. For a while, the enormous budgets of the studios were put completely at the service of directors. In many cases this artistic freedom led to commercial success.

The death of auteur freedom is often linked to one film: *Heaven's Gate* (Michael Cimino, USA, 1980), which virtually bankrupted United Artists. Generally, the failure of this film is attributed to Cimino's complete lack of regard for either the costs of the film or the needs of a mass audience.

Worksheet 5 The age of Hollywood auteur freedom

Worksheet 6 *Heaven's Gate*: Auteurism uncontrolled?

These worksheets encourage students to explore some of the key features of this period.

To access worksheets and other online materials go to **www.bfi.org.uk/tfms** and enter User name: **auteur** and Password: **te2103au**.

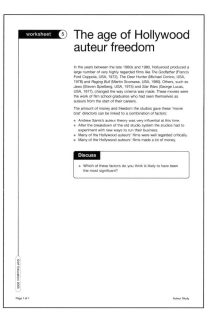

1 of 2 pages

High-concept and independent Hollywood

After something of a decline in the 1980s, Hollywood film's increasing success since the start of the 1990s has been associated strongly with the high concept – a corporate approach to filmmaking that can be compared to the way genre was used during the studio era. Essentially, these are films based around a single, simple idea, drawing together various genres and using stars like Schwarzenegger overtly as 'brands'. Key high-concept directors include James Cameron, Jan de Bont and the Wachowski brothers. There is a thorough, accessible summary of the high concept in the *bfi* resource pack, *Film as Product in Contemporary Hollywood* by Roy Stafford and Nick Lacey.

Potential issues for considering the problems of auteur study and the high concept can include:

● Like genre, the high concept predetermines the style and narrative of film. Is there scope for auteur originality within it?
● Some high-concept directors, such as Cameron, are very powerful because of their commercial successes. Does this give them auteur freedom?

At the same time, there has also been a resurgence in distinctive Hollywood auteur filmmaking. Inspired by Quentin Tarantino's success with *Reservoir Dogs* (USA, 1992) and *Pulp Fiction* (USA, 1994), studios are once again willing – with some caution – to put money into less obviously commercial projects. This has led to higher production values and wider distribution for auteurs like P T Anderson, Christopher Nolan and Wes Anderson.

For more material on this topic see online student notes **Why is Tarantino allowed to remain independent?** at www.bfi.org.uk/tfms.

● 3. Authorship and genre

Worksheet 7 Auteur vs genre: Comparing two gangster genre endings

Use this worksheet and supporting student notes, focusing on *The Godfather* (Francis Ford Coppola, USA, 1972) and *Angels with Dirty Faces*, to encourage students to compare genre-critical readings of film with auteurist approaches. It is not essential to show either film in full, but if you have time, we have found that both are generally very popular with students.

To access worksheets and other online materials go to **www.bfi.org.uk/tfms** and enter User name: **auteur** and Password: **te2103au**.

For a very useful introduction to genre study, we strongly recommend chapter 4 of *Film Art* by Bordwell and Thompson and the *bfi* resource pack, *Film Genres: An Introduction* (2002). For a developed discussion, going beyond A Level, the 'History of Genre Criticism' in *The Cinema Book*, edited by Pam Cook and Mieke Bernink is extremely useful, and Rick Altman's excellent *Film/Genre* (1999) is becoming the standard text.

Authorship and genre are alternative ways of organising films into a critical context.

- The auteurist looks for aesthetic quality in film; the genre critic looks for patterns.
- Auteur criticism sees film as the product of creative artists; genre criticism sees it as the result of social forces.
- Auteur criticism is more 'artistic' and 'subjective'; genre criticism is more 'scientific' and 'objective'.

Common directions for auteur study in relation to genre are:

- Can a director make genre films but still be an auteur?
- Can a genre be an auteur signature?
- How do auteurs imprint their personalities on genre films?

The best way for students to gain confidence with these concepts is through studying films which can be explored from both perspectives. *The Godfather* is a product of the Hollywood auteur period and a gangster movie.

Using auteur-based approaches with genre film

To begin with plot and character, *The Godfather* seems to be a story of romantic individualism. These were the kinds of narratives that the *Cahiers* favoured in their criticism and, when they became directors, in their filmmaking. Often in their work, the central character symbolises the artist–outsider: in other words, s/he stands for the director. This film is completely focused on its central character, Michael Corleone (Al Pacino). He is a romantic individualist who, through great adversity, gradually comes to terms with his own identity and his place in the world.

The film and its director fit quite neatly into Sarris's auteur theory. According to Peter Biskind (1999), Coppola was a key player in the 1970s age of auteur freedom, which Biskind believes to have been the 'last golden age of movies'. As a director, Coppola exerted a great deal of personal control over the making of this film and was not just a studio puppet. For example, he co-wrote the script with Mario Puzo. In subsequent interviews (on the DVD extras, for example) he has often spoken of his expectation at the time of making *The Godfather* that the film would not do well. He was, in other words, thinking of an artistic realisation rather than of pleasing the audience.

The account Biskind gives of Coppola's filmmaking approach (pp152–57) reinforces this. The director seems to have spent a great deal of his time in conflict with both his own crew and with studio executives. He insisted on sticking to his own unpopular decisions and was frequently very close to being fired, not least because the performances of his actors and the low-level lighting on the dailies ran counter to the expectations of his bosses. Later on, Coppola realised his dream of setting up his own production company, Zoetrope. It should be clear that on the criterion of struggling for independence against studio 'classicism', Coppola scores many auteur points.

As for the body of work we would expect from an auteur, Coppola's career has been somewhat patchy. But looking at the best of his other films, for example *The Godfather Part II* (USA, 1974), *The Conversation* (USA, 1974) and *Apocalypse Now* (USA, 1979), we can see a thematic unity. These are all films about the nature of America, dealing explicitly with ideas of moral choice and personal destruction.

The Godfather is widely recognised as a significant piece of film art, in which form and content are very beautifully managed. In other words, it fits with Sarris's idea that an auteur film contains 'interior meaning'.

A purely auteur-based study of *The Godfather* would look at this film as a key text in Coppola's career as a whole. It might consider personal issues, such as the influence of Roger Corman or Coppola's friendships and rivalries with other directors, including George Lucas. The distinctive thematic and stylistic characteristics of Coppola's oeuvre would also be taken into account, as well as the way in which he has worked with actors and writers. In the end we would have an assessment of the film itself and as a part of Coppola's auteur identity. We would assess its place within his body of work. Biskind's description of the film certainly follows this line. Here, for example, he identifies what he sees as Coppola's auteur signatures:

> Coppola relied on his DP to frame the shots. Coppola's strengths were writing dialogue, storytelling, and working with actors, not visual composition. (Biskind, 1999, p157)

Using genre-based approaches with auteur film

Pauline Kael, who hated everything Sarris stood for, loved *The Godfather*. In her *New Yorker* magazine column she described it as 'the best gangster film ever made in this country' (quoted in Biskind, 1999, p163). Instead of discussing the film in the context of Coppola, a genre critic (like Kael) discusses it in the context of other gangster movies. How does this change our understanding of the film?

We would have to consider the whole history of the gangster genre, going back to the 1930s to compare *The Godfather* with the likes of *Little Caesar* (Mervyn LeRoy, USA, 1931) and *Angels with Dirty Faces*. These films all shared some key characteristics, including the following thematic and narrative elements:

- There is always an interest in the way gangsters tend to belong to oppressed ethnic minorities.
- The attitude to violence and criminality is invariably ambivalent – both are condemned in the script, but also clearly provide the audience with thrills.
- Criminals are shown as monsters, but also as human beings – particularly the central character.
- The central character is destroyed by his life of crime – it must lead to his death.
- These films lead to debate about the amount of moral choice the central character has – the audience is asked to consider: Is he just a victim of circumstances, or could he have behaved any differently?

These are not the only shared characteristics, but are enough to start considering how *The Godfather* fits into its genre. Its narrative and thematic structure clearly includes the first four points. As for the fifth, Michael Corleone becomes an amoral, power-crazed criminal, but is not punished with death. At the end of the film, he is at the peak of his power. This would never have happened in a 1930s' gangster movie, in which the gangster always had to be shown the error of his ways before dying for his sins. The online resources explore some ways of looking at these sequences.

From a genre-analysis point of view, we would see this development as entirely the product of its time. The films simply dovetail with the social attitudes of the times in which they were made.

Bringing auteur and genre together

The Godfather can be illuminated both by a genre reading and an auteurist one. It is also possible to combine these approaches and suggest that Coppola, as an auteur, found new creative possibilities in the gangster genre, just as the studio age auteurs had done.

Biskind is quite keen to see *The Godfather* as the work of a genre auteur. Here, he compares Coppola's work to that of the more obviously unconventional and hippyish Dennis Hopper and Robert Altman:

> ...unlike the anti-genre exercises of Hopper and Altman, Coppola, like Bogdanovich with *What's up Doc?*, breathed life into a dead formula, looking forward to the genre gentrification of Lucas and Spielberg to come. (p164)

On the other hand, he holds on to the idea of Coppola as an artist shaping his personal vision, saying that the director,

> connected to the themes of *The Godfather* (and its sequel) in a profound way ... in Michael's pact with the devil lies the tale of Coppola's uneasy relationship with the studios, and his brave, if stumbling, attempts to build his own independent power base. The *Godfathers* would be the most personal films Coppola would ever make. (ibid)

As we have tried to establish throughout this guide, the auteurist perspective says that what is good and/or interesting about a film is the way it reflects an individual creative personality. The genre-critical approach may be based on one of two lines of approach. It may see film as social practice and be interested in how a genre fits into the ideologies and expectations of the society that produced it. Or, as in the writing of Pauline Kael, it may look for aesthetic quality in individual films in terms of what they do with the conventions of the genre.

The Godfather can be analysed from both types of genre perspective, as well as from an auteurist point of view, and these approaches will mostly complement each other. Actually, this is quite common in Hollywood cinema. Some other student-friendly auteur/genre films to consider discussing, each compared with a more typical example of the genre, are:

- *Reservoir Dogs* (heist) compared with *The Thomas Crown Affair* (Norman Jewison, USA, 1968).
- *Donnie Darko* (Richard Kelly, USA, 2001) (high school romance) compared with *10 Things I Hate About You* (Gil Junger, USA, 1999).
- *Following* (Christopher Nolan, UK, 1998) (film noir) compared with *The Maltese Falcon* (John Huston, USA, 1941).
- *Near Dark* (Kathryn Bigelow, USA, 1987) (vampire) compared with *Dracula* (Terence Fisher, UK, 1958).

In the first of each of the above pairs, there is a strong auteur identity working within genre conventions. The second is more strongly representative of the genre than of its director.

Genre and non-Hollywood auteurs

When considering world cinema, or American independent filmmakers, the situation becomes more complex. Such films may belong to their own genre families, such as the Hong Kong martial arts movie, or they may be strongly anti-genre, for example Ozu's Zen-influenced Japanese cinema or the work of the Dogme '95 group. Alternatively they might borrow from Hollywood genres but re-form them. Films of the latter type can be used in class to emphasise the creative power of the auteur who works outside the studio system, or outside America.

For example, a very conventional, though competent, piece of genre work such as *The Shawshank Redemption* (Frank Darabont, USA, 1994) can be compared with an independent film like *Down by Law* (Jim Jarmusch, USA, 1986). Much of Jarmusch's work begins as genre: *Dead Man* (USA, 1995) is a Western; *Ghost Dog: The Way of the Samurai* (USA, 1999) is a hitman/gangster film. Put these films next to any Hollywood product in the same genre, and the differences of style, story, characterisation, cinematography and attitude are obvious.

Similarly, a comparison between *A Chinese Ghost Story* (Siu-Tung Ching, Hong Kong, 1987) and *Poltergeist* (Tobe Hooper, USA, 1982) or *La Haine* (Mathieu Kassovitz, France, 1995) and *Boyz N the Hood* (John Singleton, USA, 1991) will show how the horror or street-gang genres have been reconstructed by non-European auteurs.

The case studies, particularly those on romantic comedy and the *Alien* franchise, are also relevant to the relationship between auteurs and the genres they work in.

● 4. Group auteurs

In his account of Hollywood, *Adventures in the Screen Trade*, the screenwriter William Goldman takes the auteur theory to task on a number of accounts. His principal complaint, however, is that auteurism simply does not describe the conditions that apply in the Hollywood production system. This, he maintains, is a collaborative medium, in which the best directors simply do a good job of drawing together the team. He expresses it in financial terms relevant to the year he wrote the book, 1983:

> Look at it logically. Studio executives are not stupid, and they are, believe it or not, aware of costs. If the director creates the film, why does a studio pay three thousand dollars a week for a top editor? Or four thousand for an equivalent production designer. Or ten thousand plus a percentage of the profits to the finest cinematographers?
> It's not because they're cute.
> And it's not because they want to. They have to. Because that's how crucial top technicians are. Crucial and creative. (1996, p101)

He is, of course, correct in this. And, although he is at pains to emphasise that he is only qualified to talk about Hollywood, the fact is that feature-length filmmaking is a group project in Japan, Sweden and the UK too. There are very few films like *El Mariachi* (Robert Rodriguez, Mexico/USA, 1992) for which the director's credits also include writer, cinematographer, camera operator, editor, music editor and sound editor. Such movies tend to be self-financed 'calling cards' by young directors wanting to make themselves a name. Other examples include Christopher Nolan's *Following* and Sally Potter's *Thriller* (UK, 1979). Even in films made with this level of apparent single-handedness there is still a lot of collaboration. As is clear from his book *Rebel without a Crew* (1996), Rodriguez worked with (unpaid) friends, including his cast, who supplied a good deal of the creative input.

Regarding *Thriller,* Sally Potter has this to say:

> Thriller... was shot with one of my hands on the sound button and the other one on the camera, and then I edited it. Under those circumstances perhaps auteur is the right word to use. But hang on, there were four performers in *Thriller*, so what was their status? Of course they gave their input too, and their input became part of the image. And what about the people who printed the film at the lab? In other words, film can never be a solo medium in the way that the novel is ... Having said that, a film is not a committee medium. It has to be steered by one person. And this is the paradox. It is a collaborative medium, but with a director. (From 'The Contemporary Auteur: An Interview with Sally Potter' by Kristy Widdicombe at http://www.bfi.org.uk/nationallibrary/collections/16+/auteur/potter/)

Sometimes authorship is overtly shared. For example, Jean-Pierre Jeunet and Marc Caro took equal directorial credit for *La Cité des Enfants Perdus* (France, 1997). However, one could argue that this ignores the significant contributions of Jean-Paul Gaultier (costume design) and the film's digital effects artists.

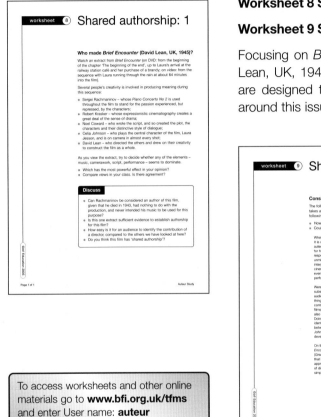

Worksheet 8 Shared authorship 1

Worksheet 9 Shared authorship 2

Focusing on *Brief Encounter* (David Lean, UK, 1945), these worksheets are designed to encourage debate around this issue.

To access worksheets and other online materials go to **www.bfi.org.uk/tfms** and enter User name: **auteur** and Password: **te2103au**.

It may be helpful to use different terms for different types of group auteurs. In *Stars* (1998, pp151–52) Richard Dyer suggests that there are four types of authorship:

1. Individual authorship – where a single voice is evident and acknowledged;
2. Multiple authorship – where many voices contribute and are acknowledged (as in *Brief Encounter*, the work of the Coens or Caro and Jeunet);
3. Collective authorship – where no single author is acknowledged for any particular element of the process and a group takes the credit. Dyer seems to be thinking specifically of leftist and agit-prop filmmaking 'collaboratives' here, since he gives the example of the London Women's Film Group.

4. Corporate authorship – where an economic institution such as a studio is the author. Dyer expands this to suggest that 'Hollywood' could be an author, where the film is generic and/or high concept, or that we could even consider films to be authored by America, or by capitalism.

This can be a good starting point for discussion. As our case study on *Alien* will demonstrate, however, a single film can encompass all four types of authorship suggested by Dyer and more.

It is worth discussing, for example, the notion of combative authorship, where the finished product is the consequence of aggressive disagreement between the parties involved in making the film. One very useful example of this is the conflict between Tony Kaye and Edward Norton on the final cut of *American History X* (Tony Kaye, USA, 1998).

While this film that may not be appropriate for younger students, the story of its production demonstrates very interestingly how films can reach their final form through disagreement as well as co-operation. Kaye's final reflection on *American History X* in an article he wrote for *The Guardian* seems to support the idea that any power the film has really derives from the creative tensions that went into its making.

> I appreciate now that I was an immature idiot, and a complete egomaniac. But I had passion. And that passion helped a young actor give the best performance of his career, and get nominated for an Academy award. I played my part in that. ('Losing It', Tony Kaye, *The Guardian* Friday Review 25 October 2002)

The whole article is a useful discussion resource, and can be accessed at http://www.guardian.co.uk/arts/fridayreview/story/0,,818065,00.html.

The idea of group authorship can be very useful as a way of exploring the artistic and/or ideological meanings either of a single film or a sequence of films. However, deciding on how authorship is attributed in each case will always be a matter for debate. Students need to learn to be open to possibilities, and to see the authorship of films as a dynamic rather than a fixed entity.

3

Case studies

In this section, we apply four major ideas from Section 2 to specific cases. This allows further exploration and provides examples of auteur study 'in action'. In terms of the WJEC Film Studies specification, Case studies 1 and 2 are more clearly aimed at the FS6 exam, while 3 and 4 lean towards auteur coursework.

Case study 1: *Alien* and multiple authorship

By the end of this case study, students should have:

- Recognised that auteur status is problematic;
- Considered a detailed example of corporate and co-operative authorship in Hollywood;
- Developed an understanding that such authorship is composed of both co-operation and conflict;
- Acquired an awareness that there is often disagreement over the retention of authorship 'credit';
- Increased their understanding of what constitutes a directorial 'signature';
- Explored the extent to which decision-making processes, particularly the choosing of personnel, are part of authorship.

They should be able to write any of these essays:

- Do you feel that Ridley Scott can be considered the author of *Alien*?
- With reference to a case study, discuss the idea that the auteur theory is not true in Hollywood.
- 'To be an auteur, a director must come close to controlling every element of production.' Discuss with detailed reference to the production of a particular film.

The nine-disc DVD box set of the four *Alien* films released in 2004 (also available as individual two-disc editions of each film) provides teachers with a superb resource for the investigation of Hollywood auteurship. Each of these four films is a chapter in the same narrative sequence; each director would seek to develop – or would already have developed – a distinctive auteur identity. Consequently, the films demonstrate similarities based on genre and seriality, but each deviates from the template in some way. They are all very alike; all very different. The films alone are sufficient to explore this issue: how a new director imposes his signature on the sequence. The extensive DVD additions provide a range of other perspectives. This case study, as well as viewing notes on several of the *Alien* documentaries, offers one way to use the set, but it is by no means exhaustive.

● Scott the auteur

All four films in this set are offered in two versions: the original theatrical cut and a new version prepared for this DVD release. A good starting point with *Alien* is to discuss Ridley Scott's brief introduction to the new cut, and to compare this with the personal contributions made by each of the other three directors. The whole idea of the 'director's cut' can be seen as Scott's invention – the first film to carry the subtitle 'The Director's Cut' was Scott's 1993 re-release of *Blade Runner*. He is a director to whom the idea of authorship is important, and who treats his own status as an auteur very seriously. This is apparent in the way he talks about his work, and also in the way others describe him. The introduction appears on disc 1 of the set, just before the Director's Cut of the film.

● Commentary

From Scott's point of view, *Alien* is an important film. It was only his second piece as a film director, it was his first project for a Hollywood studio and it made his reputation. In particular, he established a distinctive 'look' for the film. Because of his design background, Scott visualised scenes very thoroughly before shooting. In pre-production, he storyboards his own films extensively. On *Alien*, he was working within a relatively limited budget, but nevertheless found ways to create an expensive, glossy look. In many of Scott's subsequent films, he invests urban and industrial settings with beauty and power. The freighter *Nostromo* in *Alien* may be seen as the first example of this aspect of his work.

On the other hand, aside from this sense of visual style, there is not much that unifies Scott's output. His films include a wide variety of genres and locations. He is a marketable 'star director', comparable with Spielberg in that audiences recognise his name as a guarantee of quality. However, unlike Spielberg, who keeps returning to the same themes (particularly childhood and innocence) in a range of genres, it is not so easy to draw out Scott's thematic interests from his films. That does not mean that he is all style and no substance; he has produced a great deal of intelligent, satisfying work. But if we apply Sarris's definition, Scott is very much like John Huston, whose career also produced an important body of Hollywood work but no clear auteur identity. Other directors of films in the *Alien* sequence had much clearer auteur signatures. If Scott is a *metteur en scène*, then perhaps Truffaut was wrong to suggest that the best work of such a director is always less interesting than the worst work of an auteur.

Of course, this is only if we define Scott as a *metteur en scène*. He has quite clearly chosen the role of auteur for himself.

In his introduction to *Alien*, Scott is very obviously seeking to stake a claim as the person with 'artistic rights' over the film. He assumes, and expects us to agree, that he is the one who can decide whether changes need to be made to the theatrical cut. The important issue, we are being told here, is whether the film satisfies Scott. The presentation of two versions of *Alien* on the same disc is an invitation to learn how the 'Director's Cut' is superior to the original presentation. His changes probably make little difference to the audience's experience of the movie, but with them and his piece-to-camera introduction, Scott is making the same sort of statement that Alfred Hitchcock used to make through his personal appearances and cameos. Barthes might well suggest that Scott is saying 'I am an auteur, the ultimate authority on this film'. Whether or not Scott is right to do so is a matter for discussion. He is not the only possible auteur of *Alien*.

● Who raises *Alien* out of its genre?

Although this case study is not focused on genre, it is important to raise the subject because *Alien* is a studio genre movie. There may be some disagreement about which genre, or genre combination it belongs to, though we favour Scott's idea that it is an 'old, dark house movie'. Certainly, audiences in 1979 were turning up to see a horror film, rather than a Ridley Scott film. It is only since Scott's career has developed that it has also become possible to consider *Alien* the work of an auteur. We know that most Hollywood auteur directors have worked within genre. As with John Ford and the Western or Hitchcock and the thriller, the auteur signature can itself be a genre.

Most critics agree that *Alien* is more than just a genre piece. Remind your students of Sarris's 'circles'. The key questions to discuss are these:

- What are the 'quality' elements of *Alien* that raise the film out of its genre?
- Is Scott responsible for these?
- Does *Alien* fit into a career path for Scott?
- Scott was not very interested in science fiction – does this make him a good or bad genre director?

Many of the DVD extras are based on an auteurist point of view, and tend to assume that *Alien* is Ridley Scott's film. Before looking at these, you can ask students if they have any suggestions as to who else might be an author of this film. A reminder here of what William Goldman had to say about the auteur theory (see p36) will be useful since you are about to discuss an example of group authorship in Hollywood. The question is: can we identify a single auteur for this film?

Since we know that Scott controls the cinematography of his films, we can rule out his DP. The remaining candidates for auteurship are:

- Dan O' Bannon and Ron Shusett (writers);
- H R Giger (design of the creature and the alien spaceship);
- Sigourney Weaver (star – arguably created the character of Ripley).

The extra documentaries on the second disc are organised helpfully into 'Pre-production', 'Production' and 'Post-production'. This allows you to work through the processes by which a Hollywood movie comes to the screen, and to watch the stages of its authorship.

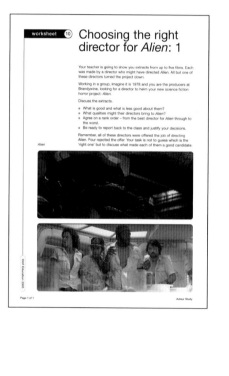

Worksheet 10 Choosing the right director for *Alien*: 1

Worksheet 11 Choosing the right director for *Alien*: 2

Worksheet 12 Who were the authors of *Alien*?

To access worksheets and other online materials go to **www.bfi.org.uk/tfms** and enter User name: **auteur** and Password: **te2103au**.

1 of 2 pages

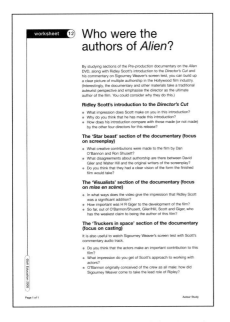

These worksheets and the supporting student notes provide a variety of activities based on these documentaries. They can be worked through sequentially or dipped into in order to raise a particular issue. In sequence, they deal with the following aspects of a film's authorship:

- The contribution of the writers;
- The contribution of the producer;
- How a director is chosen;
- The importance of visual designers;
- Casting and the contribution of the actors;
- Composition and choice of music.

The following sections of the *Pre-production* documentary ('Star beast', 'The visualists' and 'Truckers in space') are particularly useful.

● Star beast

This section deals with the writing of the screenplay and raises some interesting issues for discussion. First we learn that the original idea for the screenplay came from Dan O'Bannon. Initially, his ideas were quite generic:

> *Dark Star* [the student film O'Bannon had made with John Carpenter in 1974] as a horror movie instead of a comedy. A scary movie on a spaceship with a small number of astronauts.

By following the creation of the film from this initial idea through to production, we can ask the question: At what point did *Alien* stop being a genre picture and become something more than that?

If there is an obvious moment when this happened, then perhaps the person who made that change can be seen as the author of the film. O'Bannon came up with the original plot. He also decided that the alien would enter the spaceship by involving a human crewmember in its life cycle. However, the plot is limited (monster kills people one by one) and the infection of a crew member was common in space fiction: on television, *Star Trek* had repeatedly used this device.

O'Bannon became friends with Ron Shusett. He wrote the rest of the script at Shusett's house. There he ditched his original title, *Star Beast*, and replaced it with *Alien*. The title was a significant contribution to the film, but is not enough to make the film O'Bannon's work. Next Shusett came up with a key idea. It was he who suggested that the alien should burst out of the chest of its first victim. This is a very significant contribution to the narrative, to the audience experience and to the reproductive/sexual symbolism which fills the completed film; and important, given what Gordon Carroll and David Giler say later in the documentary.

The completed script was almost sold to Roger Corman's production company. If they had bought it, *Alien* would have been shot as a low-budget, exploitation movie. If you can find any films from the Corman stable from this period, such as *Island of the Fishmen* (Italy, 1979) or *Up From the Depths* (Philippines/USA, 1979), show an extract to give students an idea of the sort of trash *Alien* could have become. O'Bannon and Shusett would have let this happen. This suggests that they did not have any clear vision of the finished picture. Perhaps this reduces any auteur status they have.

In the end, the script was bought by Brandywine Productions, a new company set up by Walter Hill, David Giler and Gordon Carroll. They saw the potential in the screenplay. What then follows is an interesting struggle over authorship. Giler and Carroll suggested that the script was terrible and needed to be completely rewritten. The 'chestburster' scene was the only thing about it that was any good, but this was so good that it sold them the script. O'Bannon and Shusett disagreed with this view. In the end, O'Bannon kept sole credit for the script, but it is clear from the documentary that Giler in particular feels that he and Walter Hill really wrote the version of *Alien* that ended up on the screen.

This section of the documentary, along with **Worksheet 12**, is an excellent basis for a discussion of the extent to which Hollywood screenwriters count as authors of the finished movie.

● The visualists

Gordon Carroll starts off this section by saying that he wanted to make *Alien* into an 'A' movie. Remember that O'Bannon and Shusset had almost sold the script to Corman, who would certainly have made a 'B' movie. This perhaps means that Carroll and his producer associates have to be given some credit for the final quality of the film. Various directors turned down the project before Ridley Scott was appointed. O'Bannon freely admits that he did not understand at the time why Scott had been given the job. Looking at the director's one previous film, *The Duellists* (UK, 1977), Carroll and the others recognised that a potent visual sense was needed to turn *Alien* into an 'A' film; O'Bannon was worried that Scott didn't have anything to do with science fiction. In the 'Production' section of the documentary, O'Bannon explains that it was only much later, when he saw some of the rushes, that he finally realised Scott's value.

Teaching notes with **Worksheets 10** and **11** at www.bfi.org.uk/tfms outline a useful classroom activity in preparation for showing this documentary.

The documentary suggests strongly that once Scott was on board, the film became much more of a visual project. Scott discusses his practice of storyboarding the whole movie in advance from start to finish and says that the original budget was doubled on the strength of his storyboards. There seems to be a strong argument here that the character and quality of the final piece was Scott's work. However, even with regard to visual design there is at least one other candidate for authorship.

Key to this film's identity are the unique monster designs by H R Giger. They were a completely unexpected experience for audiences of the time. Unlike anything ever seen previously in a Hollywood movie, these startling designs became central to the undercurrent of symbolic sexual violence that makes *Alien* so disturbing and effective. Giger also saved Scott from the problem Spielberg had faced on *Jaws* (USA, 1975), which had to keep its monster off screen because it was so unconvincing.

However, Giger was brought to the project by Dan O'Bannon. If Giger has a major share in the authorship of the film's visuals, then does O'Bannon not also? Had it not been for him, Giger would not have designed the creature or the alien spacecraft, and the character of the finished film would have been very different.

● **Truckers in space**

Before considering this material, discuss the extent to which students feel that the performances of the actors make a contribution to the meaning and character of the film. The Hitchcock line that actors are merely 'cattle' can be explored. Do students agree? As John Hess explains with regard to the *Cahiers* auteur critics,

> [They] considered acting and particularly the direction of acting one of the most important aspects of the director's job. In fact they even made up the title directeur d'acteurs to indicate a director, such as Elia Kazan, who was especially noteworthy for his work with actors. (From La politique des auteurs (part one): 'World View as Aesthetics', *Jump Cut* 1974 at http://www.ejumpcut.org/home.html)

These documentaries contain conflicting messages in relation to Scott's work with the actors. He suggests himself that he knew that the visuals were going to occupy most of his attention, so he needed a cast who would require little in the way of support. Evidently, he was behind the camera himself a great deal of the time, taking on the role of director of photography. It is also suggested (by Sigourney Weaver) that once, when Scott thought John Hurt's performance was not up to scratch, he did not feel confident enough to confront such a well-regarded British actor. This was, of course, very early in Scott's career. Because these interviews were carried out many years after the making of the film, there is some conflict of memory. Tom Skerritt, who played Dallas, says that the film was all about the alien and the actors had to find their own characters. Harry Dean Stanton (Brett), however, remembers being surprised when each actor was given 'five or six pages' of background from Scott, establishing total life histories for their characters.

The overall impression given in this documentary is that Scott was not, on *Alien* anyway, a *directeur d'acteurs*. However, this is a well-cast film, and Scott, with Mary Selway and Mary Goldberg, chose well. In the commentary track on Sigourney Weaver's screen test, Scott tends to emphasise the importance of the fact that it was he who chose her for the role. However, he could never have cast her, had an important decision not been made earlier in the pre-production process. As Ron Shusett explains, the script was written with a male crew in mind, but at the last moment, he and O'Bannon added a statement that any of the characters could be either sex. This was not a matter to which they had given much thought. O'Bannon also says that because the alien itself presented so many problems in the writing, he had not developed the characters much. At the time of conception, he imagined directing it himself.

At some time in the development process, the character of Ripley became female. According to the documentary, it was probably Hill or Giler who made that decision but nobody seems to remember with much confidence. This is an issue students need to consider not only in relation to the first film, but to the franchise as a whole. The female central character, and the performances of Sigourney Weaver in that role, have been among the most distinctive and, at the time of the first film, unexpected elements of the franchise. Yet nobody knows for certain who made Ripley into a woman. When authorship is as shared as it seems to have been in *Alien*, some of the key creative decisions can happen without anyone noticing.

As the *Alien* franchise continued, Weaver, whose star power was developing strongly, took more and more control over her character and over the films as a whole. An accomplished stage actress, this was her first film role. It is possible to argue that *Alien* presented at least as clear an indication of her future identity as an artist as it did of Scott's, possibly more so.

To demonstrate that the struggle over authorship did not end with pre-production and production, it is also worth exploring the documentary segment, *Future Tense*. See **student notes: The music of *Alien*: An example of combative authorship** at www.bfi.org.uk/tfms.

● The franchise

It is unlikely that any class would have time to explore all four films, though this would make for an interesting personal study. Having established the corporate nature of much Hollywood authorship through a close analysis of *Alien*, you can use extracts from the remaining films to explore the importance of directorial 'signature', even in Hollywood. Many of the personnel involved in the creation of the first film also contributed to others. Brandywine produced all four films; Giler and Hill provided story for *Aliens* and wrote the screenplay for *Alien³*; Weaver starred in all four as Ripley; Giger's alien designs were used, with modifications, in all four films, and he provided more designs for *Alien³*, which was also edited by Terry Rawlings. The basic plots of all four films are also driven by the lifecycle of the alien, as invented by O'Bannon and Shusett. Nevertheless, each is completely distinctive from the others in look and feel, and each develops a new thematic element. *Aliens* is a high-octane war film from the director of *The Terminator* (James Cameron, USA, 1984); *Alien³* (David Fincher, USA, 1992) explores imprisonment and masculinity (its director would go on to make *Se7en* (USA, 1995) and *Fight Club* (USA, 1999); *Alien Resurrection* (Jean-Pierre Jeunet, USA, 1997) focuses on human biology, the third film in a row to do so by the director of *Delicatessen* (France, 1991) and *City of Lost Children* (France/Germany/Spain, 1995).

Multiple authorship can eventually result in too many cooks spoiling the broth. A good, if gruesome, example of this is the sequence showing the death of the mutated alien near the end of *Alien Resurrection*. Before looking at this sequence, ask students to consider how many auteurs have been involved in bringing the narrative to this point. There are many: O'Bannon, Shusett, Giler, Hill, Scott, Giger, Weaver, Cameron, Fincher and Ferguson all made significant contributions before *Alien Resurrection* even entered pre-production. Onto those, we now add Jean-Pierre Jeunet, the director, and Joss Whedon, the writer, both talented artists.

Whedon had worked successfully as a TV comedy writer, and was about to become a very big name through his creation of the TV series *Buffy the Vampire Slayer*. Jeunet had made two highly original films in French with Marc Caro, both combining science fiction and period settings with grotesque, surreal narratives. Had they been given the freedom to create a completely fresh project, it might have resulted in something remarkable. The *Alien* series, however, was already too strongly pre-defined by other auteurs. The series had varied considerably, but at its centre was the alien without feeling and a tone of unrelenting seriousness. The screenplay of *Alien Resurrection* was the product of a writer most highly valued for his snappy dialogue and his ability to bring humanity to monsters; the director was a quirky fantasist with a taste for surreal humour and carnival. Consequently, the film is full of wrong notes.

The death of the monster is grotesquely comic and ironic. It is sucked out into space through a very small hole burned into the ship with a gobbet of its own saliva. The point of realisation that it has been murdered by Ripley, who is effectively its mother, is marked by a look of puppyish sorrow from the monster. Compare this scene to Giger's original comment that he preferred his creatures not to have visible eyes so that they would appear more threatening. It is clear that Jeunet and Whedon took authorial control of the film in a way that Fincher failed to do with *Alien³*, and Jeunet has pronounced himself very happy with it. Audiences were generally less pleased, as were reviewers, most of whom compared it unfavourably with the first and second movies.

Case study 2: Genre and authorship – romantic comedy

By the end of this case study, students should have:

- Considered a detailed example of the way genre and authorship interact;
- Compared the levels of auteur freedom inside and outside contemporary Hollywood;
- Experienced the ways in which a director can subvert genre conventions;
- Explored the idea that auteur status is often dependent on conforming to dominant expectations regarding gender and sexuality;
- Increased their understanding of what constitutes a directorial 'signature'.

They should be able to write any of these essays:

- Do filmmakers have to create 'serious' films to be considered auteurs?
- With reference to a case study, discuss the tension between auteur and genre.
- What are the costs to the auteur of working within the mainstream industry and do they outweigh the benefits?

If a filmmaker is to be considered an auteur, we would expect him/her to do something new and interesting with any genre s/he works within. In this case study, we look first at a clear case of *metteur en scène* filmmaking: the Jennifer Aniston romcom vehicle, *Picture Perfect* (Glenn Gordon Caron, USA, 1997). Having established the characteristics of a typical romantic comedy, we then consider the more original approaches to the same genre of Australian writer/director P J Hogan in *Muriel's Wedding* (Australia, 1994), *My Best Friend's Wedding* (USA, 1997) and *Unconditional Love* (USA, 2002).

Since contemporary directors often present problems in terms of students' access to critical material in print, this case study also operates as a model of auteur research using only the two types of source most likely to be available to students. These are the internet (for reviews, interviews and data at www.imdb.com) and the DVD extras (which are extremely limited for these three films). We also assume a basic grasp of the main auteur theoretical positions.

● Background to the genre: *Picture Perfect*

Picture Perfect has been selected because it came out in the same year as *My Best Friend's Wedding* and is easily available on DVD, but you can adapt the ideas here to any conventional romcom.

You may choose to show this film in its entirety (preferred) or to work with the synopsis (see **student notes** at www.bfi.org.uk/tfms) and extracts identified in

Worksheet 14 A genre-driven romantic comedy: *Picture Perfect*

worksheet 14 A genre-driven romantic comedy: *Picture Perfect*

(Glenn Gordon Caron, USA, 1997)

If possible watch the whole of *Picture Perfect*. You should pay particular attention to the following eight sequences:

1. The head, titles and establishing sequence from the very start up to the point where Kate outlines her 'Number two, and that ain't bad' campaign idea. (Approximately 0.00.00 to 0.05.40)
2. The last part of the wedding party, from Kate standing outside the hall, through her first meeting with Nick, and concluding with her sitting on his knee. (Approximately 0.11.00 to 0.16.00)
3. Sam's tender words to Kate after they have had sex. Ending with his words, 'Fabulous, my reputation remains intact,' when he realises that she is asleep. (0.36.00 to 0.37.30)
4. Kate's proposition to Nick in a Boston diner, and his response. (Approximately 0.40.00 to 0.44.00)
5. Kate talks to Nick about her father. (Approximately 0.52.00 to 0.54.00)
6. The fake break up, and its aftermath up to Nick's exit in a taxi. (Approximately 1.05.00 to 1.09.30)
7. Kate finds Nick's parting gift of a Cinderella watch, followed by her speech to her colleagues. (Approximately 1.23.30 to 1.26.40)
8. The final moments and first kiss (Approximately 1.32.00 to 1.35.00)

Activity

As you watch each sequence, consider, and make notes about, the following aspects of the film:

- What is the intended effect of the sequence on the audience?
- What does the sequence tell you about the characters?
- What moral or ideological messages are being presented through the sequence?
- How does the sequence fit into the narrative?
- What aspects of the sequence are traditional for the genre?
- What aspects of the sequence are not traditional for the genre?

Page 1 of 1

Auteur Study

● Using the resources

Worksheet 13 The genre well

Use this worksheet to introduce the three strong influences on the creation of a genre film. These are:

1. The 'well' of genre characteristics as used in previous movies of the same genre
2. The changing expectations of the audience
3. The creativity of individuals (auteurs) involved in making the film

To access worksheets and other online materials go to **www.bfi.org.uk/tfms** and enter User name: **auteur** and Password: **te2103au**.

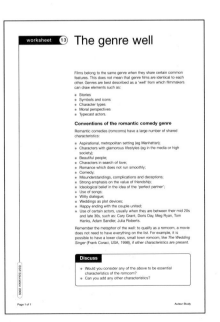

worksheet 13 **The genre well**

Films belong to the same genre when they share certain common features. This does not mean that genre films are identical to each other. Genres are best described as a 'well' from which filmmakers can draw elements such as:

- Stories
- Symbols and icons
- Character types
- Moral perspectives
- Typecast actors.

Conventions of the romantic comedy genre

Romantic comedies (romcoms) have a large number of shared characteristics:

- Aspirational, metropolitan setting (eg Manhattan);
- Characters with glamorous lifestyles (eg in the media or high society);
- Beautiful people;
- Characters in search of love;
- Romance which does not run smoothly;
- Comedy;
- Misunderstandings, complications and deceptions;
- Strong emphasis on the value of friendship;
- Ideological belief in the idea of the 'perfect partner';
- Use of songs;
- Witty dialogue;
- Weddings as plot devices;
- Happy ending with the couple united;
- Use of certain actors, usually when they are between their mid 20s and late 30s, such as: Cary Grant, Doris Day, Meg Ryan, Tom Hanks, Adam Sandler, Julia Roberts.

Remember the metaphor of the well: to qualify as a romcom, a movie does not need to have everything on the list. For example, it is possible to have a lower class, small town romcom, like *The Wedding Singer* (Frank Coraci, USA, 1998), if other characteristics are present.

Discuss

- Would you consider any of the above to be essential characteristics of the romcom?
- Can you add any other characteristics?

Page 1 of 1

Auteur Study

Referring to the worksheets and to the film, students should be able to find plenty of evidence of the conventionality of this film. If you are watching the movie as a whole, you need to be aware of the points at which each key extract begins and remind students to pay particular attention to these.

Student notes: The work of a *metteur en scène* at www.bfi.org.uk/tfms can be used as a model response to a genre film, perhaps after students have written their own accounts of *Picture Perfect*. Alternatively it can act as source material for a discussion of the film. Do they agree with this rather harsh criticism?

● *Muriel's Wedding*

Background

It should be obvious from the outset that this film is very unlike *Picture Perfect*. Before viewing, it is worth discussing P J Hogan's auteur credentials.

- He both wrote and directed this film.
- Substantial elements of the film were autobiographical.
- The film was made outside Hollywood (in Australia).
- The budget for the film was not large (approximately $3m).
- The film was independently produced.
- The initial pre-production budget was supplied by Film Victoria, a state agency for the promotion of Australian film.
- Most of the production money for the film came from a French company, Ciby2000, who had previously funded directors with strong auteur identities, such as David Lynch, Jane Campion and Mike Leigh.

In some respects, therefore, the production context of *Muriel's Wedding* can be compared to that of Lynne Ramsay's films, *Ratcatcher* and *Morvern Callar*, discussed in Case study 3. At this stage in his career, Hogan appears to fulfil many of our expectations of the independent auteur.

Commentary

After viewing the film, students should discuss the extent to which it seems to conform to the romantic comedy genre template. The obvious key elements here are the focus on a search for love and marriage, the central female character and the assumption of a female audience. At first sight, it must be admitted, the film offers far more that is outside the genre than is inside it. Its locations and characters are the very opposite of aspirational; the heroine, who is neither beautiful nor particularly sympathetic, does not end up with a man. In a 2002 *Sight and Sound* article, however, Andy Medhurst has suggested that *Muriel's Wedding* is about an unrealised lesbian relationship between Muriel (Toni Colette) and Rhonda (Rachel Griffiths). Viewed in this way, it looks much more like a romcom. This is the story of a couple who begin a relationship, fall apart and then realise that they belong together. There is a certain amount of comedy.

For this reading to work, it does not matter whether we agree with Medhurst that the Muriel/Rhonda relationship is a 'romantic' one. Romcoms are frequently not so much about romance, as they are about making the right choice of lifetime friend. Returning for a moment to *Picture Perfect*, the character of Nick (Jay Mohr) in that film is the 'right man', but he is never represented as sexually interesting to Kate or to the audience. In fact, in that film, it is the Kevin Bacon 'wrong man' character, Sam Mayfair, who is sexually attractive.

In the romcom world, sex does not enable relationships; instead it is often a problem to be beaten by characters, and only after this can they become and/or stay soulmates. For further evidence, see *Manhattan* (Woody Allen, USA, 1979) and *When Harry Met Sally* (Rob Reiner, USA, 1989). Considered in these terms, *Muriel's Wedding* is definitely a romantic comedy, not just because it is a comedy about romance but because it fits the romcom's genre expectations.

The original twists on the genre, which we would associate with an auteur director, now begin to accumulate. This is a romcom in which

- The central relationship is between two women: one confined to a wheelchair; the other plain, overweight, and mentally unstable;
- The central character is at best morally ambiguous. She steals from her own family, defrauds the immigration department and plays a major part in causing her mother's suicide;
- Nobody has a glamorous job. This is a world of dry-cleaners, video shops and petty, corrupt local councillors;
- The plot includes terrible tragedies: Rhonda's cancer, Betty's death;
- The locations are either grim (Porpoise Spit) or tacky (Hibiscus Island);
- Popular music is used ironically to criticise the idea of romance.

Had Hogan continued to work in his native land on self-scripted, smallish-budget movies, we would have had no difficulty in seeing him as a particular type of auteur. However, his next career move was to Hollywood and a studio genre film.

● *My Best Friend's Wedding*

Background

After *Muriel's Wedding*, Hogan relocated to Hollywood. Since the studios are happiest with reproducible genre products, we might expect a significant reduction of his auteur power in this new context, and for his first Hollywood movie to be much more generic, much less 'auteurish' than *Muriel*. According to Sarris's model of authorship, he would then fail the 'career' test.

To understand the next step in Hogan's career, it is important to consider what personal cachet he had built up at that time. With the exception of the 1970s' auteurs, directors in Hollywood have mostly had to prove themselves commercially viable before being allowed to take real control of their own projects. Hogan was nowhere near the status of a Ford or a Hitchcock.

Muriel's Wedding had certainly been successful, grossing $15m in the US and $42m in the rest of the world on its first cinema release: a significant profit on its $3m budget. But, to put that into context, a $3.5m budget film of a few years later, *The Full Monty* (Peter Cattaneo, UK, 1997), would take $45.8m in the US, and $198m in the rest of the world. In other words, Hogan had built up a decent reputation, but he was not going to Hollywood to write his own pay cheques or be given total auteur control.

This leads to an interesting moment in the career of any independent director. What happens when s/he joins the mainstream? Some, like Quentin Tarantino, are allowed to do more or less what they like with the company's money, and therefore develop a strong auteur identity. **Student notes: Why is Tarantino allowed to remain independent?** at www.bfi.org.uk/tfms is a useful point of comparison here.

Hogan's first job in Hollywood was as a second unit director on a film written and directed by his wife: *How to Make an American Quilt* (Jocelyn Moorhouse, USA, 1995). Shortly afterwards, he was attached to a Julia Roberts project, based on an original script by Ronald Bass. This film was being produced by Tristar, a subsidiary of Columbia associated with Hollywood auteurs such as Woody Allen. A director for Tristar could perhaps expect more free rein than those working for other production companies, but Hogan was very much the new kid on the block. Looking at the film, how well does his auteur identity withstand its clear genre status?

Commentary

My Best Friend's Wedding is not the type of film conventionally associated with auteurism, or with 'quality' filmmaking. However, as Andy Medhurst suggests, our ideas about what constitutes serious and important cinema are often quite sexist:

> Look again at most of the Best or Greatest Films lists and they palpitate with testosterone – men running newspapers, men with guns, men in the Mafia, men leading the Bolsheviks, men in space, men not giving a damn, men tormented by existential angst, men riding camels – need I go on? ('But I'm Beautiful', *Sight and Sound*, July 2002 at http://www.bfi.org.uk/sightandsound/2002_07/feature02_ButImBeautiful.html)

The sorts of films he refers to here are films that have given their directors auteur status. Compared to *Lawrence of Arabia* (David Lean, UK, 1962), *Citizen Kane* (Orson Welles, USA, 1941) or *The Godfather*, *My Best Friend's Wedding* will seem a lesser thing, both in style and substance, and its director is unlikely to be considered an auteur. This film is a comedy, aimed at women, but then so was *Muriel's Wedding* and that, Medhurst argues very convincingly, was a work of some depth with big themes and powerful characterisation. Can we make a similar case for Hogan's next film?

At first sight, we might think that Hogan, so distinctive and personal in his previous film, has simply swallowed the Hollywood bait and churned out a genre movie. Here is the evidence for that view:

- The film was marketed as a romantic comedy.
- It was produced in Hollywood at considerable expense ($46m).
- It has a glossy, expensive look.
- It was a star vehicle (for Julia Roberts).
- The settings and lifestyles represented are glamorous and aspirational.
- Heterosexual romance, true love and marriage are all treated as ideologically 'correct'.
- There is an unproblematic happy ending.

All the above are typical of the romantic comedy genre. None of them can be applied to *Muriel's Wedding*. However, there is also evidence of a set of auteur signatures beginning to form. There are connections between the films, including the following:

- The female central character suffers from a romantic fantasy which seems close to mental illness and causes her to mislead and damage those around her.
- In the end, she recognises her mistake and becomes a more complete person.
- A single popular composer is used repeatedly (Abba in *Muriel's Wedding*; Bacharach and David in *My Best Friend's Wedding*). Performances of these songs by the characters form important set-pieces.
- The actress Rachel Griffiths appears in both films.
- In both films the central character 'ends up with' a sexually unavailable friend, rather than the romantic object of affection. In both cases, this is represented as the most complete and correct ending.
- Both films have a strong sense of visual style.
- Both films alternate between realist and ironic modes of address.

Because *My Best Friend's Wedding* was a film by the director of *Muriel's Wedding* and seems to share some characteristics with that earlier piece, this opens up the possibility that it is an auteur film. Looking at the two movies together, the spectator is encouraged to consider what else they might share.

The thematic elements of *Muriel's Wedding*, and its toughness of approach, may also be present in *My Best Friend's Wedding*. If we did not connect it with the earlier film, we might not look for these elements. In other words, these two films together provide support for the idea that an auteurist approach can illuminate a film and increase our understanding of its qualities.

Worksheet 15 P J Hogan's personal style

Some students experience difficulty in recognising irony, while others can spot it but struggle to explain it. It is very helpful, therefore, to offer a good working definition of irony in film because it is important in the modes of address adopted by many contemporary directors. We have provided one on this worksheet, along with other key terms to describe Hogan's auteur approach.

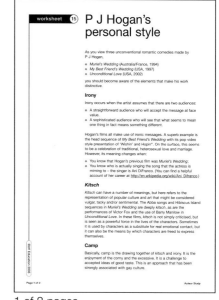

To access worksheets and other online materials go to **www.bfi.org.uk/tfms** and enter User name: **auteur** and Password: **te2103au**.

1 of 2 pages

The ironic self-awareness of *My Best Friend's Wedding* is obvious from the opening sequence. This deliberately saccharine, parodic performance of the Baccharach and David song 'Wishin' and Hopin'' signals to the intelligent audience that the basic ideology of the romantic comedy is not accepted here. Although we see the song mimed by an actress whose look is strongly reminiscent of Doris Day (Raci Alexander), the voice we hear is that of Ani Difranco, a radical folk singer strongly associated with lesbian and feminist politics. This alone should be enough to demonstrate that the film belongs to the same family as *Muriel*. It is the audience's first contact with the narrative, and offers a critical judgement on everything that follows. After it, even apparently crowd-pleasing, aspirational moments like the final wedding sequence with the happy couple driving off between fountains are regarded less positively than they first appear. An intelligent audience will not forget that Kim (Cameron Diaz) has abandoned her education and career to achieve this moment of glamour.

Throughout the film, there is a tension between the need to give the audience what it likes (in the manner of *Picture Perfect*) and resistance to the gender conventions of the romcom. A useful activity is to ask students to look at user comments for this film at www.imdb.com, which indicate that audience reactions are very mixed. Frequently, it is obvious that what users dislike about *My Best Friend's Wedding* is deviation from the genre template. A morally disreputable central female character; a male lead who is not especially charismatic; the 'heroine' not getting the man; the fundamentally anti-romantic tone are all subjects for complaint.

On release, the film enjoyed box-office success, taking almost $127m in the USA and $148m in the rest of the world. Part of this success can be accredited to Julia Roberts' star power, some to Rupert Everett's winning performance as George. Hogan's direction, however, is also a key element in the character of the film. He works through a narrative that challenges the conventions of the genre and as far as possible emphasises those challenges. Yet simultaneously, he offers the romcom audience enough of what it expects to keep it watching.

As with any genre film, the expected audience can take some share of the authorship. In this case, it was not just a matter of prediction by the writers and producers: a number of changes were made after test screenings, including a rewrite of the ending. Overall, the film is a good example of the ways in which a creative perspective has to be shifted in order to fit the needs of the industry, but it is not just a template genre movie.

In the case of *My Best Friend's Wedding*, Hogan can be seen as subverting a genre from within, where in *Muriel's Wedding* he had attacked it from outside. In both cases, the result was success with audiences.

● *Unconditional Love*

Background

After the massive popularity of *My Best Friend's Wedding*, P J Hogan might easily have made another romantic comedy with another big star. *The Wedding Singer* (Frank Coraci, USA, 1998) and *The Wedding Planner* (Adam Shankman, USA, 2001) both proved that there was plenty of commercial life in the wedding-themed romcom. Instead, his success gave him leverage to develop a very individual project, co-written and produced by his wife, Jocelyn Moorhouse.

Unconditional Love (USA, 2002) turned out to be such an oddity that the studio decided not to risk giving it a US theatrical release. It had limited distribution in Europe and Australia in 2002 with little promotion and some unfriendly reviews. Consequently, it did badly at the box office. However, since then the film has developed a smallish, but enthusiastic and growing, cult following, thanks to cable showings and a DVD release in 2003.

Commentary

Many sources and listings classify *Unconditional Love* as a romantic comedy, though it is even further from obviously belonging to that genre than *Muriel's Wedding* was. The central relationship between Grace (Kathy Bates) and Dirk (Rupert Everett) is founded not on attraction to each other, but on their mutual love for the late Victor Fox (Jonathan Pryce). The film does not contain one example of a conventional physically attractive heterosexual character: all the leads (a frumpy housewife, a bad-tempered gay man and an uncompromising dwarf) are, in one way or another, outsiders.

The possibility that this film is another of Hogan's variants on the romcom is worth discussing with students, as are the reasons for New Line's nervousness about giving it a US release. In fact this movie seems only to have been exhibited in US cinemas on two occasions: at the Philadelphia Lesbian and Gay Film Festivals in July 2003 and July 2004, where it was extremely well received.

> Playing to a packed house in Philadelphia, the audience clapped, screamed, cheered, and at the end, applauded the credit roll; unheard of in American movie theatres today. (www.imdb.com, user comment)

Romantic comedy has always attracted a sizeable gay audience; the closet homosexuality of one of the genre's key figures, Rock Hudson, was an open secret inside and outside Hollywood, and *Pillow Talk* (Michael Gordon, USA, 1959) with Hudson and Doris Day is regarded as a classic of gay cinema. So, did New Line consider *Unconditional Love* 'too gay' for the mainstream? This is an issue that can be explored in relation to the specific presentation of Everett's character, but also to the narrative, style and attitudes of the film as a whole, which are strongly reminiscent of the gay writer Armistead Maupin's *Tales of the City* series. Looking back over these three films, we might conclude that Hogan's distinctiveness lay in bringing the gay subtext of romcom much nearer to the surface. With *Unconditional Love*, perhaps he made this too obvious for the studio.

With its ironic tone, love of absurdity, strong sense of kitsch and camp, a plot centring around unattainable dreams of love and a resolution in which outsider characters find long-term happiness in friendship, *Unconditional Love* picks up Hogan's signatures and amplifies them. It is not a film that one could be expected immediately to take seriously and yet it does aggressively challenge Hollywood's ideas about the sorts of stories and characters that can appear in a mainstream movie. We can see Hogan using the auteur power he had developed through *Muriel's Wedding* and *My Best Friend's Wedding* to bring this production into being. Clearly, however, the auteur signatures here were so strong that they were seen by the producers as harmful to the film's commercial prospects. In these circumstances, the production companies take the course of action that they think is likely to recoup the most, or lose the least, money.

It is interesting to compare this experience with those of other more illustrious directors than Hogan: Welles with *The Magnificent Ambersons* (USA, 1942), or Ridley Scott with *Blade Runner* (USA, 1982). As Hogan said in an interview with the *Sydney Morning Herald* on the set of his next film, *Peter Pan* (USA, 2003),

> The fight never stops.... You fight to keep the complexity of the work; you fight to stop them dumbing it down. They're scared of anything different because it may put somebody off. (Garry Madox, 'Off to Never Never Land', 12 December 2003)

The battle with the studios is fought repeatedly by auteur directors and the battleground is often genre.

Case study 3: Lynne Ramsay as director

The aims of this case study are

- To offer an example of an auteur study – the director, Lynne Ramsay;
- To enable students to develop the skill of close analysis;
- To enable students to develop the skills of research and evaluation.

● Introduction

Born in Glasgow in 1969, Lynne Ramsay studied photography at Napier College in Edinburgh and cinematography and direction at the National Film and Television School. Her graduation film, *Small Deaths* (UK, 1996)*,* and two subsequent shorts, *Kill the Day* (UK, 1997) and *Gasman* (UK, 1997), won various awards, including two at the Cannes Film Festival, but it wasn't until her debut feature, *Ratcatcher* (UK, 1999), that she achieved widespread critical acclaim.

Ratcatcher tells the story of 12-year-old James Gillespie, who accidentally kills another boy, Ryan, by pushing him into a canal. Set against the background of the refuse-workers' strike in Glasgow in 1973, we watch James trying to come to terms with his crime, his attempts at escaping his environment and the friendship he forms with 14-year-old Margaret Anne.

In her second feature, *Morvern Callar* (UK, 2002), Ramsay also uses a death as a catalyst for the plot. An adaptation of Scottish beat writer Alan Warner's 1995 novel, the eponymous heroine, played by Samantha Morton, discovers her boyfriend has committed suicide, claims authorship of his novel, and, using the money, escapes to Spain with her best friend, Lanna. On the surface, Morvern, who Ramsay describes as 'a Camus type of character' (*indieWire:*, 2000), shows neither grief nor guilt, but, like the central character of Albert Camus's *L'Étranger* (1942), her actions pose existential questions regarding morality and death.

So far, the media have been quick to recognise her as an original filmmaker. Peter Bradshaw has described her as one of the very few with the conviction to be taken seriously as an auteur, in the highest and most fully unapologetic sense of the world … that rarest and most unfashionable of things: an artist. (*The Guardian*, 2002)

● Individual style

A film style can be defined as the individual characteristics we associate with a director's technique and can refer to cinematography, editing, sound and *mise en scène*, but also to such aspects as narrative technique and the use of actors. Identifying an individual style is dependent on a viewer's previous experience of film. A viewer will inevitably compare a film with what s/he has already seen. Alternatively, a viewer with a wider knowledge and understanding of film might identify influences on a director. If this is the case, s/he might judge the film in relation to those influences, for example, whether a director's style is sufficiently different to call his or her own.

But is style really important? Yes, when you consider the production context of most films. In such a high-cost, high-risk industry, personal expression will always be marginalised in favour of safer models (genre, star vehicles, the high-concept film). An auteur has the ability to offer the viewer a new way of looking at the world and, in turn, challenge the homogenous worldview presented by more conventional Hollywood narratives. But as André Bazin suggests, if too much emphasis is placed on individual style, there is a danger that the content of the film is overlooked and that social and historical aspects are obscured.

Lynne Ramsay has suggested that her style is something she developed in her short films, *Small Deaths*, *Kill the Day* and *Gasman* (*indieWire:*, 2000). An analysis of these films is revealing. We have focused on the following aspects:

- Narrative
- Cinematography
- Editing
- Sound
- *Mise en scène*
- Use of actors

Narrative

There are no obvious storylines in *Small Deaths*, *Kill the Day* and *Gasman*. Ramsay does not impose a story onto her characters; instead, she lets it evolve organically from a situation. She has described a film as being made from a series of 'moments' (Ramsay, 1999, pxii). *Small Deaths*, for example, chronicles three moments in Anne-Marie's life; and in *Gasman*, events seem to unfold naturally as they would in a 'day-in-the-life-of' documentary. There is not a beginning, middle and end as we would expect from a more conventional narrative, but Ramsay has rejected the idea that there is no plot in her films (Guardian Unlimited, 2002). *Small Deaths* is about the death of Anne-Marie's innocence; and on closer examination of *Kill the Day* and *Gasman*, a three-act structure can be identified. In *Kill the Day*, the conflict is between the burden of the past and the escape offered by addiction, but the resolution to give up taking drugs is not only temporary but made unclear by an absence of time codes – we cannot be certain whether it occurs in the past or the present. In *Gasman*, too, the conflict between Lynne and her half-sister is only temporarily resolved when she decides not to throw the stone at the end. In each case, the story isn't explicit, but takes place on a psychological level.

Cinematography

Ramsay studied photography at Napier College in Edinburgh and cinematography at the National Film and Television School, so camera position, movement, framing and composition are important aspects of her work. At first look, however, Ramsay's camerawork has an artless, documentary quality to it. She uses a handheld camera to show the violence of the boys in 'Holy Cow'* and the chaos of the party scene in *Gasman*. The action does not seem to be staged for the camera; figures move in and out of the frame as they would in reality; and subtle tilts and pans and lens movements mimic the way a documentary follows the action. On closer analysis, however, signs of authorial control are evident. In *Small Deaths* and *Gasman*, the low camera position has the effect of creating a child's point of view; tightly framed shots are used to create a feeling of entrapment and claustrophobia; and the shifts in focus between foreground and background in the telling of the story are only possible through careful composition. Furthermore, focusing on the details of everyday life, Ramsay often leaves the viewer to imagine what is happening outside the frame. For example, in *Gasman*, instead of a conventional one-shot of the girl putting on her shoes, she focuses only on her legs. This use of an open frame helps us to realise how much the body and voice of her mother intrude on her personal space.

Editing

Ramsay has expressed an interest in the 'rhythm of things' (*indieWire:*, 2000) and has compared 'the language of cutting' to 'music' (*Interview*, 2000). In all her films, she adapts the pace of the editing to match the action. Sometimes she allows the audience 'breathing space' (Ramsay, 1999, pxi) to contemplate the psychological resonance of a particular image; and sometimes she speeds up the flow of images to create a psychologically dramatic moment – the ending of 'Holy Cow' and 'The Joke'*, for example. These psychological

---

* These are extracts from *Small Deaths*, available on the DVD of *Ratcatcher*.

moments in her films are further emphasised through other editing techniques: the use of slow motion (the fly buzzing around the light bulb, the boy falling into the canal, and the drug dealer in the car in *Kill the Day*); or the insertion of an image to show what a character is thinking (the shot of the cabbage field, representing an imaginative escape, in the same film). Similarly, Ramsay rejects the rules of continuity editing (shot/reverse shot, eye-line matches, etc) in favour of a more impressionistic montage of images.

Sound

Although auteur theory emphasises the visual aspects of style, Ramsay has consistently noted how sound is undervalued as a technique in filmmaking, commenting once that 'sound is the other picture' (Guardian Unlimited, 2002). In all her films, ambient sound is used to convey emotion or create atmosphere; and Ramsay often prioritises off-screen over on-screen sound in the telling of the story. Sometimes sound is used to indicate what a person is thinking. In 'Ma and Da'*, Anne-Marie's image blurs and we hear the sound of children playing, indicating her desire for escape; and in the second part of *Small Deaths*, as Anne-Marie gazes at the dying cow, we hear again the sound of the boys killing it. Dialogue is naturalistic and often improvised, but doesn't function in the way dialogue normally functions – the exposition of narrative or character. It is often 'superfluous' (Ramsay, 1999, pxi) and contradicts what an actor is communicating through body language.

Mise en scène

Ramsay hardly ever works with sets because she likes 'to get the feeling that you're in the real place' (*indieWire:*, 2000). Instead, she shoots on location, mainly in working-class areas of Glasgow. Interiors tend to be cramped; ambient lighting serves to emphasise this lack of space; and shadows and silhouettes are common. It is worth noting too Ramsay's unusual attention to colour (the vibrant colours of 'Holy Cow', in particular, conveying the freedom of the two girls), or lack of it (the institutional white of *Kill the Day* that seeps into the other scenes); and her ability to create a period setting ('Ma and Da' in *Small Deaths* and *Gasman*) without resorting to stereotype.

Use of actors

The use of unknown or non-professional actors creates a sense of realism in the film; an actor's star image is not allowed to detract from the character. Similarly, improvisation lends a realistic quality to the action. Ramsay comments:

---

* This is an extract from *Small Deaths*, available on the DVD of *Ratcatcher*.

the kids' party in *Gasman* was a real party that I shot like a documentary. Only some of the dialogue was fictional. It was a really exciting day because all the kids started fighting and went bananas – it's all on film. I like that element of spontaneity. (Interview, 2000)

To explore these ideas in a classroom context, see Case study 3 teaching notes and student notes on Lynne Ramsay's individual style at www.bfi.org.uk/tfms.

● **Themes**

In Section 2, we suggested an auteur may be defined as a filmmaker who makes films with similar themes – a definition which has the potential to enhance or limit our understanding of a film. In the case of *Ratcatcher*, Ramsay has acknowledged it 'has similar concerns – in terms of subject matter and I guess in terms of style, theme and characterization' to her shorts, but, in relation to themes such as childhood, she doesn't 'want to be pigeonholed as a filmmaker' (Ramsay, 1999, ppvii–viii).

We have identified the following themes in the film:

● **Childhood** On one hand, Ramsay, who describes *Ratcatcher* as being about 'the death of childhood', seems to be highlighting the damaging effect the adult world can have on children; but she is also interested in childhood because 'your opinions are not yet set' and you are 'like a blank canvas, in terms of the direction you can take for good or bad'. Interestingly, Ramsay says as a filmmaker she tries 'to look at things from a child's point of view' (Ramsay, 1999, ppviii–x).

● **Death** The sudden death of what we think is the main character is shocking and leaves us thinking that anything could happen. The event haunts James throughout the rest of the film. Indeed, the film is about James coming to terms with his guilt, but also his own mortality.

● **Entrapment and escape** Undoubtedly, the housing estate signifies a new beginning. It is a place where James can play away from the canal, the boys of the estate, his family and Maryhill. Ramsay has said of the scene:

It's his journey to another place, a new home, a place of solace. He is alienated in his own environment, where he sees his own bleak future written in the faces of the people who surround him. He fantasises of belonging in a beautiful place that is very pure and clean, a place he feels he doesn't deserve, due to his guilt over his own actions. (The Roddick Profile, 1999)

See **Worksheet 16**
Lynne Ramsay: Themes

This worksheet and supporting student notes indicate how you can explore these themes in more detail and examine the idea of authorship in the film.

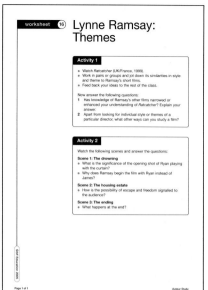

● Authorship of *Ratcatcher* and *Morvern Callar*

Ramsay constructs her auteur identity, not only through her style and themes, but also through signature shots and a self-conscious creation of 'a body of work'. As we have seen from the above activity, the scene at the new housing estate includes two 'signature' shots – shots which are repeated in *Morvern Callar* at similar points in the narrative. The first is of James in one of the new houses and is repeated in *Morvern Callar* in the scene on the rooftop cemetery. We see James leaning against a wall in the house on the right of the frame. The camera pans slowly from right to left until James appears on the left-hand side of the frame. In *Morvern Callar*, the camera moves in the opposite direction. In both cases, the shot breaks rules of continuity, it doesn't 'make sense'; it is a trick, a surrealist jolt, drawing attention to the illusion of cinema and the presence of Ramsay behind the camera.

Ratcatcher: Trickshot

Second, the shot of the window framing the field in *Ratcatcher* is repeated in *Morvern Callar* where Morvern sits next to a window looking onto the sea – both express a desire for escape and freedom. As James climbs through the window into the field, it is as if he is climbing into a fantasy world. Ramsay comments:

> [W]hen James [...] goes for the first time into the field for me it felt to me like this boy's never seen a field, so we should heighten it, because in his mind it's completely unreal. (indieWire:, 2000)

Ratcatcher: The possibility of escape

But these shots are not the only links between the two films. The ending of *Ratcatcher*, for example, is ambiguous. Two contradictory scenes are offered to the audience for consideration. In the first scene, we see James jumping into the canal – we assume to drown himself. In the second scene, we see the family carrying furniture across the field to the new house. The credit sequence returns us to a slow-motion image of James underwater. But is his suicide real and his escape imaginary? Or is his suicide imaginary and his escape real? Certainly his suicide can be explained psychologically: on his second visit to the house, he discovers he has been locked out; despite telling Margaret Anne that he loves her, she continues to let the boys of the estate abuse her; and Kenny, who now kills the animals rather than looks after them, reveals that he saw James push Ryan into the canal, perhaps foreshadowing the disclosure of his secret. On the other hand, the man and woman who came from the council to inspect their flat would no doubt have left with the impression that they needed new housing. In Ramsay's view, the ending is 'open to interpretation'.

It isn't, however, the end. Narrative closure is simply deferred until her next film, *Morvern Callar*. In Alan Warner's original novel, the identity of the writer who commits suicide at the beginning remains a mystery; he is referred to only as 'He' or 'Him', as if he were God. In her adaptation, however, the name of her boyfriend on the computer screen is James Gillespie – the 'hero' of *Ratcatcher*. It follows then that James doesn't commit suicide at the end of *Ratcatcher* and indeed escapes, but still kills himself years later in a relationship with Morvern. What we can now say is the happy ending of *Ratcatcher* is the unhappy beginning of *Morvern Callar*. His escape is only temporary.

Furthermore, in attributing authorship of the novel to James Gillespie, Ramsay is signalling that she is the author of the film. The roots of the film lie just as much in her work as in Warner's. She is not a *metteur en scène* translating the novel into film, but an auteur with her own vision. Indeed, changes in the story indicate a more direct form of authorial control. For example, in omitting the fact that in the novel Morvern is pregnant because '[i]t suggested you grew up by getting pregnant' (Guardian Unlimited, 2002), Ramsay is bringing her point of view as a female director to a novel that is told from the point of view of a woman but is nevertheless written by a man.

Interestingly, Ramsay has described *Morvern Callar* as 'very "death of the author"' (Gerald Peary, 2003) and saw Morvern's boyfriend 'as Alan Warner really' (Guardian Unlimited, 2002). Certainly our response to her actions is a test of how much we cling to the notion of authorship; in the existential world of the film, posthumous fame is seen as meaningless. But Ramsay is more interested in asserting her own authorial voice than she is in questioning Warner's. As she says:

> the postmodern cut-and-paste job, that's just not me. Maybe it's a bit naïve, but I still think you can be original. (Ramsay, 1999, pxiv)

To develop these ideas with a class, see teaching notes at www.bfi.org.uk/tfms.

● Authorship and tradition

François Truffaut originally defined the auteur in opposition to 'la tradition de la qualité' that dominated French cinema at the time. In the case of Lynne Ramsay, her work has been seen in the context of the British tradition of social realism, exemplified by the films of Ken Loach and Mike Leigh. So is Ramsay an auteur or a social realist? Key points have been summarised below:

Ramsay as auteur:
- Ramsay uses the refuse-workers' strike to create a psychological backdrop for James, symbolising his repressed guilt and mental breakdown. It is just as much a symbolic landscape as a realistic one.
- The film portrays an isolated individual. This emphasis on subjective, as opposed to objective, reality is emphasised through point-of-view shots and *mise en scène*. Ramsay comments:

> I think the images in *Ratcatcher* generally came from trying to work out
> where we are psychologically with the characters. (indieWire:, 2000)

- There is a distinct visual style to the film.
- The narrative device of killing off who we think is the main character (Ryan)
  in the opening scene and following his killer (James) instead is clear sign of
  authorial control, or what David Bordwell refers to as the narration's
  commentary – an artistic narrative that draws attention to itself (Wexman,
  2003, pp42–50).
- The realism of the film is punctured by moments of fantasy – in particular,
  Kenny's mouse, Snowball, flying to the moon and the dream-like quality of
  the final scene.
- Ramsay has acknowledged autobiographical 'details' in the film indicating a
  personal approach to filmmaking (*indieWire:*, 2000), including a boy she
  grew up with who tried to send a mouse up into space (*Interview*, 2000).

Ramsay as social realist:
- Setting the film during the 1973 refuse-workers' strike anchors the film in a
  social and historical reality, thus highlighting the poor housing conditions in
  Maryhill during that time.
- The film portrays an individual who exists as part of a community, thereby
  emphasising the importance of the social.
- The film has a documentary quality to it. Cameras are often handheld;
  Ramsay makes use of available sound and light; with the exception of the
  canal, the film is shot on location; Ramsay uses unknown and non-
  professional actors; and performances are sometimes improvised.
- The story unfolds naturally as it would in a documentary.
- The story of a working-class boy alienated by his environment, and his
  attempt to escape that environment, echoes Ken Loach's classic British
  social realist film, *Kes* (UK, 1969). The two films are set within three years of
  each other and have iconographical similarities.
- Ramsay's own working-class background lends a certain authenticity to the
  film.

This apparent conflict between individual authorship and social realism
illustrates the earlier debate between Truffaut's auteur polemic and Bazin's view
of film as a recorder of social or historical reality. The question is whether
Ramsay's individual style interferes with the social message of the film. Ramsay
herself has played down the genre elements in *Ratcatcher*:

> A lot of people have misconstrued this film as social realism and I don't
> think it is. I try to avoid some of the clichés of that. [...] It's more like two
> opposing styles. (indieWire:, 2000)

She goes on to say that although she respects established filmmakers like Ken
Loach and Mike Leigh for presenting 'an alternative view of British culture' to

period dramas and British comedies made for US audiences, ultimately she found that style 'sort of strained' and tried to stand out against it.

See **Worksheet 17 Lynne Ramsay: Auteur or social realist?** and supporting student notes.

To access worksheets and other online materials go to **www.bfi.org.uk/tfms** and enter User name: **auteur** and Password: **te2103au**.

● **Creative control**

So how is Lynne Ramsay able to maintain creative control in an environment that consistently prioritises economic concerns over artistic ones? As early on as film school, she realised it was a choice:

> I felt that a lot of the scripts there were calling cards for the industry; I didn't feel that people were there for three years taking risks and being experimental. It felt like you had to have a slick product at the end. It was a time when it was really hard to get work – it was before *Trainspotting* … (Guardian Unlimited, 2002)

She is certainly aware of the economic pressures to make

> something that was prepackaged or marketed to a U.S. audience like a cuddly British comedy or a period drama. (indieWire:, 2000)

and the aesthetic pitfalls of 'plot-driven' films centred around 'stereotypes', describing them as 'bland and homogenous' (*The Telegraph*, 2002). So far, she has successfully avoided the trappings of the star system, although working with Samantha Morton in *Morvern Callar* saw leanings in that direction. Similarly, in *Morvern Callar*, she designed sound 'to avoid that MTV pop promo feel' typical of the high-concept film (Guardian Unlimited, 2000).

In interviews, Ramsay comes across as uncompromising and cynical. In her debut feature, for example, she had to work hard to resist studio control:

> When I was doing *Ratcatcher*, I heard a lot of, 'Yeah, we really love your short films, but could you just change the whole way you work and cast some name actors?' I like working with small crews, documentary-style, and I remember thinking, What are all these fucking people doing here? They said, 'Oh, you're a first-time director with a first-time crew, you need all the support you can get.' Every single thing was a battle. I was absolutely exhausted by the end of making that film. I didn't know if I ever wanted to work on another one. (*Village Voice*, 2002)

Similarly, in the middle of making what would have been her third feature, an adaptation of the Alice Sebold's bestselling novel *The Lovely Bones* (2002), Ramsay commented:

> Suddenly you get a barrage of phone calls saying, 'Gee, we really loved *Ratcatcher.*' I'm cynical enough to know that the American agents are calling because we've got a bestseller on our hands. You've got to keep your feet on the ground or you go crazy. I don't want to become a director for hire. (Guardian Unlimited, 2002)

As she has added elsewhere, one way of maintaining creative control is to work within a low budget but make each shot look like a million dollars (BBC4, 2002). Despite her complaints, however, it is probable that working with the BBC and Lottery-funded Pathé has allowed her greater artistic freedom than, say, a Hollywood studio.

Having said this, she also sees film as collaborative. In terms of her relationship with Samantha Morton, the only real 'star' in her films to date, she has accepted 'you can't dictate as a director' (Guardian Unlimited, 2000). Ramsay's preference for improvisation has allowed her actors freedom without compromising her own artistic vision.

To introduce the students to the idea of creative control and develop research and evaluation skills needed for their auteur studies, see additional teaching notes at www.bfi.org.uk/tfms.

● Conclusion

In our opinion, Ramsay is the author of her films, but also an auteur. She has fought for creative control and this has allowed her to express her own style and themes over a number of films. She has tried to distance herself from the British tradition of social realism, but her films are really a result of these 'two opposing styles'.

Significantly, however, she is no longer involved in the adaptation of *The Lovely Bones* as the project has been taken from her and passed to Peter Jackson, a director who is well known for his willingness to work with very large budgets. Perhaps this is a sign that auteur freedom in Hollywood still has to be earned with box office success.

Case study 4: Dustin Hoffman as actor–auteur

The aims of this case study are

- To offer an example of an auteur study – Dustin Hoffman as actor–auteur;
- To analyse the 'conflicts' the actor faces in Hollywood;
- To introduce Method acting;
- To begin the students' auteur studies.

● Introduction

An actor can be a popular choice for students doing auteur studies. It shouldn't be assumed, however, that the actor is evaluated in the same way as a director: individual style, thematic concerns, etc, are not necessarily useful criteria in assessing performance. Instead, an actor–auteur might be defined as one or more of the following:

- A talented or 'great' actor;
- An actor who is the principal source of meaning in a film;
- An actor who creates individual characters as opposed to types;
- An actor who has creative control over his/her performance, but also of such aspects as casting and image;
- An actor-director.

To introduce these definitions to a class, see additional teaching notes at www.bfi.org.uk/tfms.

This difference in approach means it is important to study an example of an actor–auteur in class. This may seem time-consuming, but on the WJEC A Level Film Studies specification can double up as the Performance Studies question on the Critical Studies paper. We have chosen Dustin Hoffman as a case study because:

- He is a talented actor;
- He is notorious for his conflicts with directors and producers;
- He is a Hollywood star;
- As he has become more famous, he has achieved greater creative control;
- He is a Method actor.

We will begin by discussing the conflict between the actor and director over authorship of a film.

● Actor versus director

The original *Cahiers* polemic saw the director as central to the creative process and the actor as secondary. For the director–auteur, a performance is one element among many in an overall design; and the director has the power to alter how a performance is received through 'cinematic' elements such as cinematography, editing, sound and *mise en scène*. Alfred Hitchcock, an auteur highly respected by the *Cahiers* critics, expressed this view when he famously compared actors to 'cattle'.

So when is an actor considered to be the author a film? According to Patrick McGilligan:

> When the performer becomes so important to a production that he or she changes lines, adlibs, shifts meaning, influences the narrative and style of a film and altogether signifies something clear-cut to audiences despite the intent of writers and directors, then the acting of that person assumes the force, style and integrity of an auteur. (Cited in Dyer, 1998, p153)

This might well describe Hoffman who is notorious for wanting to change lines, improvise, and 'shift meaning' in a scene, often resulting in conflict with the director. Whether Hoffman's contribution amounts to 'something clear-cut to audiences', however, can be assessed through an analysis of the opening scene from *The Graduate* (Mike Nichols, USA, 1967) when Benjamin Braddock's parents throw a graduation party in his honour. See additional teaching notes at www.bfi.org.uk/tfms.

Benjamin's discomfort at the party betrays his antipathy to the hypocritical bourgeois society it represents. Hoffman conveys this discomfort through his stiff posture, the aversion of his eyes, the hesitations in his voice, speaking in a monotone, and his increasingly desperate attempts at smiling. But this discomfort and claustrophobia are also conveyed through cinematic techniques. The long take of Benjamin leaning against a fish tank traps Hoffman in the frame; his father's entry sheds a harsh light on his face; and, sitting down, he partly obscures Benjamin from view. As he is eventually led downstairs by his parents, the camera comes to rest on a painting of an unhappy clown – a reflection of how Benjamin is feeling. The sense of claustrophobia is intensified through Nichols' use of the handheld camera following Benjamin into the party, where he is jostled back and forth by its members within a series of tightly framed shots, and, finally, through the loud voiceover of his mother reading from his college yearbook. All this is in contrast to the soothing green of the pool he stares at from his bedroom and the soothing green of the fish tank with its gentle bubbling sound.

So who is the author of the scene? *The Graduate* is a good example to use precisely because there is already disagreement. Jeff Lenburg, for example, argues that Nichols 'sometimes strives for unnecessarily artsy effects' and that Hoffman's 'knowledge of the comic vocabulary' is 'crucial' because 'despite the witty dialogue, there is nothing inherently funny in the plot or situations' (1983, p35). On the other hand, Ronald Bergman concludes that Hoffman 'is directed within an inch of his life' and we don't see 'Dustin's personality breaking through the rigid mask Nichols has constructed for him' (1991, p67). Hoffman himself agrees with the latter:

> If there is any victory in this film it's not mine. It has nothing to do with me. The film belongs to Mike Nichols [...] Nichols knew every colour, texture and nuance he wanted and worked like hell to get it. Of course I resented it. (ibid, p62)

One–nil to the director?

This conflict between the actor and director is explored more explicitly in *Tootsie* (Sydney Pollack, USA, 1982). The fact that Hoffman is playing an actor already invites an autobiographical interpretation, but this is confirmed by other similarities between him and the character of Michael:

- They were both unemployed theatre actors before making it on screen;
- They both have womanising tendencies;
- They are not 'in this business to make money', as George Fields puts it, but for their art;
- They are both talented actors;
- They are both hard working;
- They are both hard work.

Michael disagrees with everyone: his friend, his agent, his director. He storms out of a play when he is told to stand up and walk centre stage before dying; and it is reported that as a tomato in a commercial he wouldn't sit down because it was 'illogical'. When he tells George he 'bust[s] his ass to get a part right', George replies,

> Yes, and you bust everybody else's ass too ... You argue with everybody. You've got one of the worst reputations in this town, Michael. Nobody will hire you.

He is the archetypal auteur, because he wants creative control.

Hoffman's own position is illustrated by the advice he has for young actors:

> Don't be afraid to be fired. Fuck it! Why be bad? The director wants you to do it a certain way, and either you don't feel that he's right or you feel that he's right but he's forcing you to be a square peg in a round hole. You can't fit in. Quit. Better to be fired than to look bad.

He goes on:

> Unfortunately, there are not a lot of good directors around. There are more good actors. Actors have to learn acting and study it. I'm not sure directors have the same kind of background always. (ibid, p45)

With this in mind, *Tootsie* is oddly self-referential. Hoffman parodies himself through his portrayal of Michael and Pollack sends up the 'troubled relationship' between actor and director by casting himself as Michael's exasperated agent. But this self-awareness exhibited in the film did not prevent a conflict between the two on set. Hoffman compared the creative process to a boxing match between him and Pollack. Pollack said,

> Every morning, we screamed at each other for ten or fifteen minutes, discussing how the scene to be shot that day would go,

and later told the film director, John Boorman, it was the worst experience of his life. When Hoffman was asked if he would work with Pollack again, he commented:

> I'd work with Yasser Arafat if I liked the script and he gave me total control. (ibid, pp189–97)

● The actor versus the Star System

The figure of the actor–auteur can also be explained in relation to the Star System. The Star System is based on the casting decisions made by producers, directors, casting managers and agents on the basis of requiring a star to ensure the success of a film; and the activities of actors, designers, public relations officers and the media in promoting a star image. It can also refer to the use of stars in the production of films and the consumption of star images by the audience (Dyer, 1998, pp9–19). The relationship an actor–auteur has with his/her star image is an uneasy one. The Star System will seek to promote the star image at every opportunity. This image is composed as follows:

● Firstly, a 'screen persona' is created through casting an actor in similar roles. This 'character' or 'type' fits efficiently into genre and high-concept formulas and is consumed by audiences who come to see a film because of the star.
● Secondly, the actor's celebrity status is projected both on and off the screen. An actor is cast in glamorous roles; and an actor's success, money and fame are foregrounded in the media. The image of the celebrity offers the audience an imaginative escape into their world and the possibility that they too might become famous.

Thus the actor becomes capital that will attract investment and a commodity to be consumed by the audience. As Hoffman says:

> Once you are in the public eye, you think you are really something. But you just happen to be a commodity they want. Success can really cripple you. (Bergman, 1991, p2)

An actor–auteur, on the other hand, will seek to create an individual character that an audience will believe in, as this illusion is the criterion against which s/he will be judged. A series of performances must therefore exhibit 'range' (see below), but an actor must also take control of casting decisions and the way s/he is presented in the media. Paradoxically, s/he can only do this through the system. The advantage of winning an Oscar for Hoffman, for example, is that 'it is a means to more power, which in turn enables you to be choosy about your scripts' (ibid, p100). Success cannot only 'cripple' an actor, it can also give an actor greater creative control.

To assess whether Hoffman creates individual characters or is typecast by the Star System, we have looked at the following scenes:

- *Midnight Cowboy* (John Schlesinger, USA, 1969): the scene where Joe Buck meets 'Ratso' Rizzo and Ratso cons him;
- *Tootsie*: Dorothy's opening scene in which she auditions for a part in the soap opera;
- *Rain Man* (Barry Levinson, USA, 1988): the scene where Charlie Babbit first meets Raymond.

See also our analysis of the *The Graduate*, pp68–70.

Midnight Cowboy: *Enrico Salvatore 'Ratso' Rizzo*

When we first meet Ratso Rizzo, a lot is conveyed through image: the greasy, slicked-back hair, sweaty face, white suit, jewellery and cigarette-end tell us he is clearly a character Joe Buck (Jon Voight) should not trust. But a lot of Ratso's character is communicated through expression (his sideways grin) and voice (his nasal New York whine). We see Hoffman eyeing up his money and sussing him out; when a woman asks for a cigarette, Ratso takes one and offers Joe a light, making it seem like he is giving when he is really taking, an illusion he keeps up throughout the film. Hoffman's – and indeed Ratso's – performance moves up a gear out on the street. The limp/swagger, the hand gestures, the explosion of anger at a taxi, the way he guides Joe with his arm and the cough are all details that help us to imagine Ratso as an individual character as opposed to a type.

Tootsie: *Michael Dorsey/Dorothy Michaels*

In *Tootsie*, Hoffman is playing two characters: Michael Dorsey, the actor, and Dorothy Michaels, the actress. It's a role within a role, a performance within a performance. (During the audition, it becomes a performance within a performance within a performance.) We aren't warned of Michael's transformation into Dorothy when we first see her on screen, so the extent to which we are fooled by Hoffman/Michael's acting in the first instance is a measure of its success. Obviously, costume and make-up are essential ingredients, but the prim walk, the patting of her hair and the pout also contribute to the illusion. Dorothy slipping on her high-heels is a momentary slip of her disguise and serves to signal Michael behind the performance. A more interesting slip is when Dorothy meets the beautiful Julie Nichols (Jessica Lange). Here, 'her' voice breaks and 'he' leers at her over 'her' glasses. During the audition, subtle facial expressions and gestures such as the nod of her head and her smile, as well as the Southern accent, reassert her character.

Rain Man: Raymond Babbitt

Hoffman researched the role of the autistic savant, Raymond, thoroughly and this is reflected in his performance by:

- His robotic shuffle;
- The way he clutches his bag for security;
- The way he wrings his hands;
- The tilt of his head;
- The monotone voice;
- The incessant talking;
- The hesitations and repetitions;
- The refusal to look at the other characters in the face.

What makes Raymond a challenging role to play is that Hoffman is playing an individual (Raymond) and a type (the autistic). If Hoffman fails to portray Raymond as an individual, he is in danger of creating a stereotype. However, communicating what Raymond, the individual, thinks and feels is precisely what the character can't do.

In our opinion, Hoffman's ability to create individual characters demonstrates his talent as an actor. His performances in Tootsie and Rain Man are superior to his performances in The Graduate and Midnight Cowboy, but The Graduate and Midnight Cowboy are better films. (The individual styles of Mike Nichols and John Schlesinger are certainly more pronounced than those of Sydney Pollack and Barry Levinson.)

Having said this, Hoffman has been cast as an outsider in all four roles; Jeff Lenburg describes Hoffman as an 'anti-hero' (1983, p11, p186). With this in mind, it could be argued that the romantic image of Hoffman as an outsider, as an auteur fighting against the system, has become part of his screen persona – a screen persona conspicuous in most performances. When we watch a Hoffman performance, we are not watching the character; we are watching Hoffman, the 'artist', playing the character. This is perhaps what Ronald Bergman identifies in his performance as the prisoner, Louis Dega, in Papillon (Franklin J Schaffner, US, 1973) when he describes it as being 'full of actorish tics':

> Next to Dustin's overacting, Steve McQueen's performance is almost naturalistic (1991, pp124–5).

An own goal by Hoffman?

● Creative control

It is no wonder that creative control is so important to the actor; for Hoffman, it has become something of an obsession. The aspects of filmmaking that an actor might try to control are:

● The performance itself;
● Cinematic elements such as cinematography, editing, sound and *mise en scène*;
● External elements such as casting and image.

An actor might specify creative control in a contract, or become a director or producer him/herself. In both cases, their success will be determined by their value as a star. Hoffman is a useful case study because he illustrates the growth of star power in modern Hollywood.

Worksheet 18 Dustin Hoffman: Creative control

> To access worksheets and other online materials go to **www.bfi.org.uk/tfms** and enter User name: **auteur** and Password: **te2103au**.

This worksheet is a reading comprehension on Hoffman's attempts to achieve creative control. The key points are summarised below.

worksheet ⑱ Dustin Hoffman: Creative control

Below are some examples of how Dustin Hoffman has sought creative control both on and off set:

● In *Alfredo, Alfredo* (Pietro Germi, Italy, 1972), Hoffman was co-producer and had equal say with the director as to how to play his role.
● In the restaurant scene of *Marathon Man* (John Schlesinger, USA, 1976), when Babe Levy (Hoffman) finds out his girlfriend, Elsa (Martha Keller), is lying to him, there was disagreement as to how Keller should play the scene. Schlesinger wanted her to be calm, but Hoffman wanted her to be emotional. To get the effect he wanted, Hoffman kicked her under the table, effectively usurping the director's role.

Marathon Man

● Around the same time, Hoffman became a partner with First Artists Productions, an independent film company set up by Paul Newman, Sidney Poitier and Barbra Streisand, allowing him creative control over the performance and editing. First Artists produced *Straight Time* (Ulu Grosbard, USA, 1978), which Hoffman began directing, but, unable to cope with the pressures of directing and performing, he eventually hired Ulu Grosbard to take over. It was not a harmonious affair. Hoffman said:

> I was doing the best work I'd ever done, and I knew the film wasn't supporting the performance.

Grosbard disagreed:

> If he's so meticulous and such a perfectionist, why had he created such an enormous mess? (Bergman, 1991, p158)

Exceeding its budget and production schedule, the film was eventually taken over by First Studios who had the final edit. Hoffman's attempt to stop distribution failed.

Ronald Bergman (1991), *Dustin Hoffman*, Virgin Books

Page 1 of 2   Auteur Study

1 of 2 pages

● In *Alfredo, Alfredo* (Pietro Germi, Italy, 1972), Hoffman became co-producer and had equal say with the director on how to play his role.
● In the restaurant scene of *Marathon Man* (John Schlesinger, USA, 1976), when Babe Levy (Hoffman) finds out his girlfriend, Elsa (Marthe Keller), is lying to him, there was disagreement as to how Keller should play the scene. Schlesinger wanted her to be calm, but Hoffman wanted her to be emotional. To get the effect he wanted, Hoffman kicked her under the table, effectively usurping the director's role.

- Around the same time, Hoffman became a partner with First Artists Productions, an independent film company set up by Paul Newman, Sidney Poitier and Barbra Streisand, allowing him creative control over the performance and editing. First Artists produced *Straight Time* (Ulu Grosbard, US, 1978), which Hoffman began directing, but, unable to cope with the pressures of directing and performing, he eventually hired Ulu Grosbard to take over. It was not a harmonious affair. Hoffman said,

> I was doing the best work I'd ever done, and I knew the film wasn't supporting the performance. (Bergman, 1991, p156)

Grosbard disagreed:

> If he's so meticulous and such a perfectionist, why had he created such an enormous mess?' (ibid, p156)

Exceeding its budget and production schedule, the film was eventually taken over by First Studios who had the final edit. Hoffman's attempt to stop distribution failed.

- *Agatha* (Michael Apted, UK, 1979) was equally traumatic. Hoffman's writer rewrote his role from cameo to lead (although admittedly it was stated in his contract with First Artists that he had to co-star). The English producer, David Puttnam, eventually quit, calling Hoffman a 'worrisome American pest'. The American producer, Jarvis Astair, summed the situation up by saying,

> Puttnam was complaining that Hoffman had too much power. He was lucky. Hoffman didn't have as much as he wanted' (ibid, pp164–5)

The film did little for Anglo-American relations.

- In *Kramer vs Kramer* (Robert Benton, US, 1979), Hoffman was granted '[f]ull collaboration' (ibid, p174) including writing and editing, and the result was a more amicable and successful venture.
- A similar deal was struck with *Tootsie* until Pollack was signed as director and producer, giving Pollack control of casting, the script, and the final edit.

Ironically, as Hoffman has achieved greater creative control, the question of authorship has become less clear. Just because Hoffman is a talented actor does not necessarily mean he is a talented writer, producer, director, casting manager or editor. Hoffman's quest for creative control has sometimes been successful (*Kramer vs Kramer*) but in the case of *Straight Time* or *Agatha* it was achieved at the expense of the film itself.

● Method acting

To introduce Method acting, see additional teaching notes at www.bfi.org.uk/tfms.

In 1958, Dustin Hoffman was accepted at Lee Strasberg's The Actor's Studio, reputedly the best acting school in New York. At The Actor's Studio, Hoffman learnt the Method, an approach to acting influenced by the writings of the Russian theorist, Konstantin Stanislavsky, and exemplified by Michael's approach to acting in *Tootsie.* On one hand, classical theorists thought that an actor should base a performance on observation or theatrical convention. Stanislavsky, on the other hand, thought the character was created from the inside out. If an actor worked on the emotional core, signifiers of character such as facial expressions, gestures, body movements, voice, position, etc, were expressed spontaneously. To do this, an actor must first identify with a character. For instance, an actor might focus on his/her motivation, or use a memory of an emotionally charged personal experience as 'a way in'. When Sandy gets locked in the bathroom in the party scene in *Tootsie,* she decides to remember the experience in case she ever has to play a scene when she is trapped somewhere. Taken to its extreme, an actor might become or live the character, an idea articulated in *Tootsie* when Michael comments, 'I am Dorothy. Dorothy is me.'

The relevance of Method acting to our discussion of authorship is twofold. First, the basic assumption of Method acting is that the actor is the origin of meaning. Emotion is created by the actor's performance, as opposed to, say, a close-up or music. It is more likely a script is adapted to suit the character than the other way around and it might even be scrapped altogether in favour of improvisation. Second, the practice of an actor using his/her own emotions to create a character is in keeping with the romantic idea of personal expression. As Lenburg notes, Hoffman's success has depended on him 'presenting portions of *himself*' (1983, p186).

Hoffman has practised the Method throughout his career. Below are some examples:

- **The Graduate** When Benjamin is trying to get a room key for himself and Mrs Robinson, he used the experience of buying condoms from a chemist in high school as a starting point for his feelings of awkwardness:

    I would always plan on a day when I felt brave and I would walk into the drugstore and see who was behind the counter. This was very important – if it was a woman I would walk right out again – I wanted someone young – a kind of 'big brother' image. I would ask for Kleenex, some razor blades and I would get to that word and I couldn't do it. (Bergman, 1991, p61)

- **Midnight Cowboy** Hoffman was even able to identify with the character of Ratso.

    It was a character that I felt to be a very basic part of me and when I read it I had that immediate connection with him. I had for many years had this feeling about myself – that I looked like that – not literally, but in an inner way I felt I did. (ibid, p76)

Hoffman used other methods, including walking with stones in his shoes to develop the limp and wearing fake brown teeth.

- *Marathon Man* To prepare for this film, Hoffman went running every morning for six months under the direction of an Olympic trainer. He also had a sauna before scenes in which he had to look tired after running. To play a scene in which Babe hadn't slept for three days, Hoffman forced himself to stay awake for 36 hours: 'I wanted to try and match that crazed state'. Famously, Lawrence Olivier, who was playing the part of the Nazi villain, said, 'Dear boy, why don't you try acting?' Although the story has since been subject to revision, it still illustrates the difference in approach between the two actors. Whereas Olivier liked 'to have everything worked out in advance', according to Schlesinger, Hoffman preferred to improvise, demonstrating the difference between the 'old school' of acting practised by Olivier and the Method practised by Hoffman (ibid, p148). A comparison between the two performances, however, does not necessarily reveal which is the 'better' approach.

- *Straight Time* Hoffman played the role of ex-con, Max Dembo. To prepare for the role, Hoffman spent eight months at prisons across the country. In the Los Angeles County jail, he went through the admittance procedure (where it was discovered he had two unpaid traffic fines) and at San Quentin Hoffman mixed with the prisoners in disguise.

- *Kramer vs Kramer* In his Oscar acceptance speech, Hoffman said, 'I want to thank divorce' (ibid, p171), indicating the extent to which he had used his recent experience of marital breakdown to get inside the character of Ted. The scene in which Ted's son, Billy, chooses ice-cream instead of steak to punish his father was derived from an incident between Hoffman and his own daughter, Jenna.

- *Tootsie* Hoffman used his own mother as a model for Dorothy. He spent 18 months perfecting both his look and performance. He would walk around New York in disguise, once making salacious remarks to the actor José Ferrer in a lift and coming on to his co-star in *Midnight Cowboy*, Jon Voight, in a similar fashion. Much to her embarrassment, he even visited his daughter at school, pretending to be her Aunt Dorothy.

- *Rain Man* To prepare for playing the role of the autistic man, Raymond, Hoffman met both autistic people and experts on autism. The challenge was, according to Hoffman, 'to bring it home and not try to do a character that is not myself'. (ibid, p231)

See **Worksheet 19 Dustin Hoffman: Method acting**

To evaluate the Method with students, see additional teaching notes.

To access worksheets and other online materials go to **www.bfi.org.uk/tfms** and enter User name: **auteur** and Password: **te2103au**.

1 of 2 pages

● **Conclusion**

So: is Dustin Hoffman an auteur? In our opinion, Hoffman is a talented actor, whose energetic approach and on-screen presence has led to a series of memorable characters, but whose egotism has sometimes resulted in Dustin Hoffman, the actor, obscuring the character he is trying to play. Although ultimately we accept Hoffman as the author of his own performances, it is more difficult to see him as the author of his films. More often than not, his attempts to control other aspects of production have been less than successful; and his better films have been those made by directors with distinct visual styles, returning us to our original notion of the auteur – the director.

Worksheet 20 Planning sheet 1

Worksheet 21 Planning sheet 2

These worksheets will help students begin their own auteur studies.

1 of 3 pages

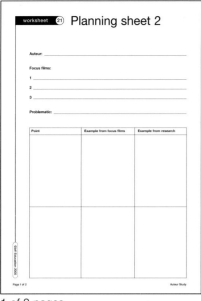

1 of 2 pages

Glossary

This is provided as a student handout at www.bfi.org.uk/tfms.

Ambient lighting
The use of natural or available light in the filming of a scene.

Ambient sound
The use of available sound in the filming of a scene.

Auteur
According to the French critics of the 1950s who introduced the idea, an auteur is a film director whose work shows him or her to be a distinctive artist. Over time, the term has come to have a wider range of meanings, and is now used not only about directors, but also stars, producers, even studios.

Auteurism
Belief in the idea of the auteur director, as introduced by the *Cahiers du Cinéma* critics in the 1950s.

Author
The person responsible for the creation of a thing. Often, but not exclusively, used to mean an artist or writer.

Authorship
1. The general condition of being an author, as in 'Alfred Hitchcock had a career in film authorship'.
2. The specific responsibility for having created a particular artwork, as in 'Authorship of *Psycho* was clearly Alfred Hitchcock's'.

Camp
1. Exaggeratedly effeminate behaviour.
2. The ironic enjoyment of kitsch artefacts.
Both meanings are strongly associated with gay culture.

Chiaroscuro
The depiction of a scene through rich, dark colours and strong use of shadow. The term originated in painting (particularly the work of Rembrandt) but can be applied to some cinematography.

Cineaste
A person with a strong interest in, and extensive knowledge about, film. Usually, the term suggests a taste for non-mainstream movies.

Continuity editing/Continuity rules/Continuity system
Editing techniques designed to create the illusion of continuity of space and time. See eye-line match and shot/reverse shot. According to Bordwell and Thompson (2004), in the studio era these techniques became a system of rules that directors had to follow.

Creatives
Creative people – directors, writers, designers, actors etc. Used as a noun to distinguish the artistic workers in the industry from the business people – producers, accountants etc, and the technical staff – camera operators, grips, gaffers and so on.

Deep focus
A technique associated with realist filmmakers in which objects in the foreground, middle ground and background are in focus at the same time.

DP/DoP
Director of Photography – sometimes credited as 'cinematographer'.

Expressionism
Specifically, a German style of filmmaking from the 1920s (see below). Generally, Expressionist film tends to emphasise subjective,

emotional experiences rather than objective 'reality' through devices like point-of-view shots, dramatic lighting and symbolism. Expressionist cinematic techniques tend to be the opposite of realist ones.

Eye-line match
A technique of continuity editing in which a subject's line of vision is matched in the next shot by what they see.

Genre
Classification of film into types, such as 'Western', 'film noir', 'melodrama' and so on.

Genre criticism
Discussion of film that emphasises its genre, and focuses on the idea of film as a social or industrial product. Often seen as opposed to auteur-based criticism, which tends to focus on film as an art form.

German Expressionism
A style of film common in Germany in the 1920s characterised by dramatic lighting, surreal settings and psychological symbolism.

High concept
An approach to filmmaking popular in Hollywood since the 1990s, typified by films like *Armageddon* (Michael Bay, USA, 1998). The key characteristics of the high concept include 'branded' stars like Arnold Schwarzenegger or Bruce Willis, big budgets, simple ideas, set-piece action sequences and a somewhat ironic tone.

Irony

The presentation of (at least) two messages at the same time: a surface message that everyone can see, and a subtext that only a 'knowing' audience will spot. The ironic subtext usually contradicts or undermines the surface message.

Italian neo-realism

A style of film common in Italy in the 1940s characterised by the use of non-professional actors, location shooting and political aims.

Jump cut

A cut the audience notices. According to the continuity system, jump cuts were to be avoided; according to the *nouvelle vague* they were essential.

Kitsch

The representation of popular culture that may be considered vulgar and/or sentimental.

Long take

A shot that continues for a long time before cutting to the next one.

Metteur en scène

According to the *Cahiers du Cinéma* critics of the 1950s, a film director who is competent, but not an artist.

Mise en scène

Literally translated from the French as 'put into the scene', this refers to the visual aspects of a film such as set, lighting, costume, etc.

Mode of address

The way in which a media text 'speaks to' its audience. The basic distinction is between direct address (character speaks straight to the audience) and indirect address (where the audience is not acknowledged). Mode of address also includes the more subtle idea of 'tone' – serious, comic, ironic and so on.

Montage

1. A sequence of shots.
2. A style of shooting and editing where the sequence is carefully assembled from fragments with no 'master shot'.
3. A sequence of images assembled to speed up the narrative of a film – for example by quickly showing the passage of many years in a character's life.

One-shot

A shot of one person – similarly two-shot and three-shot.

Open frame

A technique which draws attention to action outside the frame.

Pan

The rotation of the camera horizontally.

Point-of-view shot (PoV)

A shot from a particular character's point of view.

Portal shot

View of events through a secondary medium – most commonly a CCTV monitor or other TV screen. For example, the scene where Thelma robs a convenience store in *Thelma and Louise* (Ridley Scott, USA, 1991) is not shown directly, but seen on a CCTV recording watched by her husband and several policemen.

Rushes

The first unedited print of a day's filming. Sometimes referred to as 'dailies'.

Screen persona

The 'character' a star brings to a film, usually through association with previous roles or exposure in the media.

Shot/reverse shot

Continuity technique used mainly for showing conversation between two characters.

Three-act structure

A common approach to writing screenplays for conventional films. In *Screenplay* (1994), Syd Field suggests a screenplay should be composed of three acts: set-up, confrontation and resolution.

Tilt

The rotation of the camera vertically.

Time code

A signifier in a film that indicates the time or date or the position of a scene sequentially.

References and resources

- **Books**

R Altman, 1999, *Film/Genre*, *bfi*

R Bergman, 1991, *Dustin Hoffman*, Virgin

P Biskind, 1999, *Easy Riders, Raging Bulls: How the Sex 'n' Drugs 'n' Rock 'n' Roll Generation Saved Hollywood*, Bloomsbury

D Bordwell and K Thompson, 2004, *Film Art: An Introduction* (International Edition), McGraw-Hill

J Caughie (ed), 1981, *Theories of Authorship: A Reader*, *bfi*

P Cook and M Bernink (eds), 1999, *The Cinema Book* (2nd edn), *bfi*

R Dyer, 1998, *Stars* (2nd edn), *bfi*

W Earle and R Stafford (eds), 2002, *Film Genres* – An Introduction, *bfi*

S Field, 1994, *Screenplay* (3rd edn), Dell

D Gerstner and J Staiger (eds), 2003, *Authorship and Film*, Routledge

W Goldman, 1996, *Adventures in the Screen Trade: A Personal View of Hollywood*, Abacus

N Lacey and R Stafford, 2000, *Film as Product in Contemporary Hollywood*, *bfi*

J Lenburg, 1983, *Dustin Hoffman: Hollywood's Antihero*, St Martin's Press/Zebra

J Nelmes (ed), 2003, *An Introduction to Film Studies*, Routledge

L Ramsay, 1999, *Ratcatcher*, Faber and Faber

R Rodriguez, 1996, *Rebel without a Crew*, Dutton/Signet

A Warner, 1995, *Morvern Callar*, Jonathan Cape

V Wexman (ed) 2003, *Film and Authorship*, Rutgers University Press

● Web sites

Aspen no. 5+6 (includes full text of Roland Barthes' 'The Death of the Author') – http://www.ubu.com/aspen/aspen5and6/threeEssays.html
British Film Institute – www.bfi.org.uk
Gerald Peary – www.geraldpeary.com
Guardian Unlimited (Film) – http://film.guardian.co.uk
indieWire: – www.indiewire.com
Internet Movie Database – www.imdb.com
Interview – www.findarticles.com
Jump Cut – www.ejumpcut.org
The Roddick Profile – www.filmfestivals.com
Senses of Cinema Great Directors –
    www.sensesofcinema.com/contents/directors/
Sight and Sound – www.bfi.org.uk/sightandsound
The Telegraph (Arts) – www.arts.telegraph.co.uk
Village Voice – www.villagevoice.com

● Films

Alien (Ridley Scott, USA, 1979)
Angels with Dirty Faces (Michael Curtiz, USA, 1938)
Annie Hall (Woody Allen, USA, 1977)
Brief Encounter (David Lean, UK, 1946)
Godfather, The (Francis Ford Coppola, USA, 1972)
Graduate, The (Mike Nichols, USA, 1967)
Heaven's Gate (Michael Cimino, USA, 1980)
Marathon Man (John Schlesinger, USA, 1976)
Midnight Cowboy (John Schlesinger, USA, 1969)
Morvern Callar (Lynne Ramsay, UK, 2002)
Muriel's Wedding (P J Hogan, Australia, 1994)
My Best Friend's Wedding (P J Hogan, USA, 1997)
Picture Perfect (Glenn Gordon Carron, USA, 1997)
Rain Man (Barry Levinson, USA, 1988)
Ratcatcher (Lynne Ramsay, UK, 1999)
Tootsie (Sydney Pollack, USA, 1982)
Unconditional Love (P J Hogan, USA, 2002)

● Television programmes

British Cinema … The End of the Affair? (BBC4, 2002)

Acknowledgements

We would like to thank all the Film Studies students at Gateway Sixth Form College, Leicester, on whom many of these ideas have been road-tested over the last four years.

Thanks to Michelle Ransome for pointing us in the direction of the *bfi* and to Vivienne Clark and Wendy Earle for their support.

David would like to apologise to Frances for ignoring her and the boys during the whole of the half-term holiday while he wrote his portions of this guide.

And Jeremy would like to apologise to family and friends who he has bored senseless by talking incessantly about films.